Drug Abuse:
Perspectives on Drugs

Robert Kaplan, Ph.D.
Professor in Health Education
The Ohio State University

WM. C. BROWN COMPANY PUBLISHERS
Dubuque, Iowa

CONTEMPORARY TOPICS IN HEALTH SCIENCE SERIES

Consulting Editor
Robert Kaplan, Ph.D.
The Ohio State University

Exercise, Rest and Relaxation—*Richard T. Mackey, Ed.D., Miami University*

Alcohol: Use, Nonuse and Abuse—*Charles R. Carroll, Ph.D., Ball State University*

Reducing the Risk of Non-Communicable Diseases—*Wesley P. Cushman, Ed.D., The Ohio State University*

Drug Abuse: Perspectives on Drugs—*Robert Kaplan, Ph.D., The Ohio State University*

Safety and First Aid—*William T. Brennan, HS.D., and Donald J. Ludwig, HS.D., Indiana University*

Smoking—*John T. Fodor, Ed.D., and Lennin H. Glass, San Fernando Valley State College*

Mental Health—*James C. Pearson, Ph.D.*

Consumer Health—*Miriam L. Tuck, Ed.D., PHN., The City University of New York*

Copyright © 1970 by
Wm. C. Brown Company Publishers

Library of Congress Catalog Card Number: 75-120072

ISBN 0–697–07328–9

Printed in the United States of America.

Foreword

Health education is more than the primary phase of preventive medicine. Beyond the prevention of disease and the amelioration of health problems is its positive design to raise levels of well-being and liberate man's potential. Directly and indirectly it enables the individual to function most productively, creatively, and humanely.

One needs health to become educated and one needs education to develop and maintain health. Nor can one make full use of his education without it. Health is vital to the attainment of goals but we cannot preoccupy ourselves seeking it or in our obsession we shall fail to integrate all aspects of our development and performance. Health is a means to ends—the ends valued by the individual and society. Favorable modifications of health behaviors are essential to the attainment of these ends.

Contemporary Topics in Health Science offers a new and individualized format. Students and instructors can select and utilize those topics most relevant or most pertinent for the time available. Independent and class study, separately or concurrently, are enhanced by their organization. In this form they also provide greater opportunity to correlate health with other subjects.

Each book offers an up-to-date realistic discussion of currently significant health topics. Each explores its area in somewhat greater depth, with less trivia, than found in many textbook chapters. But they are designed to do more than merely present information. Within each are to be found more than partial explanations of facts. They are written by authors ranked by his professional peers as an authority in his field. They encourage the exploration of ideas, development of concepts, identifying value judgements, and selecting from a range of alternatives to enhance critical decision-making.

ROBERT KAPLAN, PH.D.
Consulting Editor

To my wife, Beverly, for her persistent encouragement and diligent typing of this manuscript.

Preface

The lyrics of popular music extol the "virtues" of the drug-induced trip. The Jefferson Airplane does "3/5 of a Mile in 10 Seconds" and "White Rabbit"; the Rolling Stones sing of "Lady Jane"; Steppenwolfe does a number simply titled "The Pusher"; The Byrds sing "Eight Miles High"; Simon and Garfunkel perform "A Simple and Desultory Phillippic" The Doors do "The Crystal Ship"; and the incomparable Beatles do "A Day in the Life" and "Lucy in the Sky With Diamonds." The list is nowhere near exhausted.

Songs of social protest have been "in" for sometime and will continue. Even the names adopted by groups are a form of breaking the mold. The Jefferson Airplane is in itself a drug term dealing with the manner of holding a marihuana cigarette. To the naive and uninitiated, these are only expressive songs of beauty, love, friendship, feelings, and escape from a hostile environment. In recent years, among the young, feelings seem to be more important than facts and ideas. Fortunately, the sound has great appeal and at least one study has shown the majority of young listeners don't seem to understand the lyrics. (Unfortunately, the loud sound is literally deafening—causing hearing loss in young adults). To others, these songs confirm the belief that the drug experience will provide the best route to the contented soul, pleasantness of mind, and the spiritual beauty of an ethereal world. The ticket for these trips? Only the price of whatever drugs may be popular and available—marihuana, LSD, amphetamines, and barbiturates—the so-called "pop drugs." These are currently the major contents of the bag of the trip-taker. (Heroin, once the drug of the "innercity" may now be going suburban.) There are more travelers on this route these days, is it your bag too? After all, what's wrong with a quiet pot party or a few pep-pills to carry you away from a tough week? Probably nothing for most of us, but for others considerable harm is possible. Which ones? That's a key question: "Will drugs turn you on or will they turn on you?"

There are many false assumptions and questions seeking answers on drug-taking. When, or whether or not to use them; can we learn how to handle drugs? Learn we must. Perhaps this book will raise more questions than can be answered but it hopes to help you answer some critical ones and make some important personal decisions. At the very least, one should have some valid information and give serious thought to the risks of experimenting with drugs. To use drugs because in some groups it is the thing to do, is hardly enough reason.

Robert Kaplan

Contents

CHAPTER 1

Drugs and Dependence

Everyone is a drug user. This is obvious particularly if we recognize how broad is the category which encompasses so many substances. Drugs are any chemical which have an effect on the human body. Since this would include foods, such a definition helps to account for the "naturalness" of drug-substances in our world. But this helps little with the modern concept of the drug problem. As medicines, drugs are substances used to treat illnesses, protect against disease and promote health. From a pharmacological viewpoint, drugs are chemical substances which influence the structure or function of living organims.

Primarily, it is how substances are used that leads to their reputations. With few exceptions, there are no "bad" drugs and "good" drugs. A hammer and chisel in the hands of a Michelangelo leads to an act of creation and beauty—in the hands of someone else perhaps to destruction. Turning for the moment to the non-medicinal substances, alcohol and tobacco, we can see that they are used, misused, and abused—concepts we will discuss shortly. As causes, directly and indirectly, of health problems alcohol and tobacco require separate volumes for discussion. Nevertheless they should be thought of as drugs.

Coffee and tea, regarded as foods, are both used and abused by many individuals. They contain mild stimulants and, as with most drugs, have side effects for some users and not others. In one case, a woman was hospitalized with mysteriously caused cold symptoms. She had a low-grade fever and suffered from chills, irritability and lack of sleep. Also, she was 20 pounds underweight. Normally, while working as a waitress, she drank 15 to 18 cups of coffee a day. In the hospital, on one cup a day, her symptoms disappeared within five days. Her problem may well have been compounded by smoking a pack of cigarettes a day and taking sleeping pills (to counteract the stimulants?). Other beverages such as tea, cocoa, and some soda pop, also peanuts and dentifrices contain xanthine alkaloids which can cause these puzzling conditions. (1) From cases such as this it can be seen that a given drug (even in controlled amounts) can cause different reactions in different people. Occasionally, at different times the same person reacts differently to the same drug.

Drug Abuse

Use, misuse, and abuse can only be somewhat clarified. Use or drug use is the term for the proper use of a drug as intended by the medical and pharmaceutical professions. (In addition, society's expectations of "proper use" must be considered.) Misuse can refer to self-medication or to the wrong application of a drug—using the wrong drug or medicine. Also, it may be failure to read and follow instructions. The term can be used if a physician might have allowed prolonged or unsupervised administration or written unlimited or refillable prescriptions. (For legally classified "dangerous drugs" the law now specifies a time limit). The term abuse is appropriate when self-medication or self-administration of a drug (usually in excessive quantities) leads to psychological or psychic dependence, and abnormal behavior, either separately or collectively. (2)

Addiction and Habituation

Because drugs are equated with "dope," dope fiends, and addicts and because the problem is complex—physiological, social, medical, economic, moral, legal and political—there are different vested interests and different points of view. The word "addict" is used pejoratively—conjuring up images of all manner of degenerates including sex fiends and homicidal maniacs. This is a false assumption. However, the concept of addiction is unclear.

It is said that people are addicted to coffee or tobacco, or some other habit forming substance: is this really an addiction? In an attempt to make a distinction in terms, in 1957, The World Health Organization's Expert Committee on Addiction-Producing Drugs, revised its definition of *drug addiction:* "a state of periodic or chronic intoxication produced by the repeated consumption of a drug (natural or synthetic). Its characteristics include:

1. an overpowering desire or need (compulsion) to continue taking the drug and to obtain it by means;
2. a tendency to increase the dose;
3. a psychic (psychological) and generally a physical dependence on the effects of the drug;
4. detrimental effects on the individual and society."

Further, the Committee attempted to distinguish between addiction and habituation with this definition of *drug habituation:* (habit) a condition resulting from the repeated consumption of a drug. Its characteristics include:

1. a desire (but not a compulsion) to continue taking the drug for the sense of improved well-being which it engenders;

2. little or no tendency to increase the dose;
3. some degree of psychic dependence on the effect of the drug, but absence of physical dependence and hence of an abstinence syndrome;
4. detrimental effects, if any, primarily on the individual."

Only a little thought is required to see there is great difficulty in objectively separating addiction from habituation. Physical dependence is characterized by increased tolerance and abstinence syndrome (severe illness or distress when the drug is withdrawn). Thus, the term "addiction" is widely used for drugs which can produce physical dependence—opiates such as heroin and morphine, barbiturates, and alcohol. Confusion is a result of the many who use "non-addicting" drugs regularly. Also the term "intoxication," though commonly used, is unclear except perhaps for alcohol abuse.

Ask heavy cigarette smokers how they react to quitting. Is there physical dependence indicated by an abstinence syndrome—more commonly called "withdrawal sickness"? How does an inveterate coffee drinker feel when deprived of coffee? When does a drug develop only psychic but not physical dependency? How can you distinguish between desire and compulsion? Do only drugs with psychic and physical dependency lead to the development of tolerance and require increasing dosages? When is it detrimental only to an individual but not society? Are quantities consumed a measure of addiction or habituation? Such questions are not easily or satisfactorily answered.

Drug Dependence

To cover all kinds of drug abuse, the WHO, in 1964, accepted the term *drug dependence*:

"Drug dependence is a state of psychic or physical dependence, or both, on a drug, arising in a person following administration of that drug on a periodic or continuous basis. The characteristics of such a state will vary with the agent involved, and these characteristics must always be made clear by designating the particular type of drug dependence in each particular case; for example, drug dependence of the morphine type, of barbiturate type, of amphetamine type, etc." (3)

It is pointed out that drug dependence is not a definition but a concept for clarification. We shall try hereafter to use the terms "dependence" or "dependent upon . . ." rather than "addiction" or "addicted to. . . ." Accordingly we can see that drug abuse in terms of those dependent upon drugs covers a wider range of society than many care to believe.

REFERENCES

1. REIMANN, HOBART A., M.D., "Caffeinism: A Cause of Long-Continued, Low-Grade Fever," *Journal of the American Medical Association,* 202: 1105-6, December 18, 1967.

1. What do you think of pop-rock music as a cause of drug abuse?
2. Do some habits resemble a form of dependence? What familiar habits might fall into this category?
3. Why does the use of the term "addiction" persist? What are its distinguishing characteristics?
4. Can you distinguish between drugs and medicines? Is there a difference?
5. Can you write better definitions of drugs and drug dependence? Try it.

2. Based on explanations in: AMA Committee on Alcoholism and Addiction, "Dependence on Barbiturates and Other Sedative Drugs," *Journal of the American Medical Association*, 193:673-677, August 23, 1965.
3. EDDY, NATHAN B., *et al.*, "Drug Dependence: its Significance and Characteristics," *Bulletin of the World Health Organization*, 32:721-733, 1965.

_~~_~~_~~_~~_~~_~~_~~_~~_~~_

CHAPTER 2

Drugs in Society

Drug abuse is a complex phenomenon—a problem, if you will. As you begin to objectively observe it, you can recognize several associated aspects such as health and medical, social, moral, legal, and economic. We can only deal briefly with these in this booklet. You are encouraged to use the references and bibliography for more extensive discussion and information.

The major factors to be considered are impossible to separate. These include the characteristics of: the society or social conditions in which drug abuse occurs; individuals who abuse drugs; and, the drugs being abused.

An Historical Perspective

The use and subsequent abuse of drugs is not new. Throughout history man has searched for relief and solutions to his physical and mental problems (as if these were separate entities) through the use of substances found in his environment, in nature. Herbs and plants— leaves, bark, and roots—and later alcohol, supplied some effective remedies and temporary relief. Many of these natural products are still in use today in refined forms. The modern pharmacist still relies heavily on nature for drugs. For example, foxglove, formerly used as a tea to treat dropsy (also known as edema meaning excessive fluid in the tissues), is today's source of digitalis, a heart medicine. South American Indians in the Andes have for hundreds of years chewed cocoa leaves which apparently helped them to withstand the cold and the pain of hardship. This area has been the main source of cocaine and its derivatives used as anesthetics in surgery and dentistry. (Illegal supplies of cocaine are still smuggled into the U.S. from South America). North American Indians chewed (and still do) the hallucinogenic cactus, peyote, as a part of religious ritual.

On the other hand, there were, and are, many natural substances used in intentionally harmful ways. Chemical warfare was used by the

5

Spartans in their seiges of cities. They burned sulphur and pitch to form sulphur dioxide. (1) Hemlock provided the extract used to poison Socrates in his "voluntary" execution. Hundreds of remedies, some effective and some ineffective, even harmful, have been handed down from generation to generation in our folklore. How many unintentional deaths occurred through the use of impure substances, uncontrolled dosages, misinformation, and the superstitions that a certain drug was good for a condition when in fact it was not? We'll never know.

Medicines and Self-Medication

From the witches' brews and alchemy to the apothecary and the modern pharmacologist and the pharmaceutical industry, we have come a long way in the use of drugs to alleviate pain, treat illness, and cure disease. With obviously growing benefit, medical science and pharmaceutical technology have continually refined older drug forms, discovered newer ones, and developed increasingly accurate medical applications. However, as with most everything, man's innovations and implements, there are hazards or disadvantages as well as advantages. Our continuing problem is to learn how to maintain a sensible balance.

Mary Poppins tells us, "A little bit of sugar makes the medicine go down." Mothers tell us, "Take this medicine, it's good for you." Pills come sugar-coated, aspirins orange-flavored, and cough syrups are chocolate or cherry flavored—all to entice children so that administering medicines is easier. Sometimes, if the instructions say take one teaspoon every four hours, someone believes it would be much better to use four teaspoons every hour—a dangerous practice. Occasionally prescriptions written for other members of the family are given to the ill without anxiety. Since the average household has about thirty medications in the cabinet, this form of self-medication is tempting.

Self-medication, though hazardous, isn't all bad. One needn't run to the physician for every little ailment but there are precautions. First, you need full information about the drug (or medicine) to be used— it's disadvantages too. This assumes you are familiar with and can recognize the signs and symptoms of those common, minor ailments which can be successfully treated. Thus, you should also be able to recognize those conditions which require the attention of a physician:

—abdominal pain that is severe or recurs periodically
—pains anywhere, if severe or prolonged more than one day
—headache, if unusually severe or prolonged more than one day
—prolonged cold with fever or cough
—earache
—unexplained loss of weight
—unexplained and unusual symptoms
—malaise (feeling poorly) lasting more than a week or two (2)

The greatest dangers of self-medication are delayed recognition of serious disease progress, and prolonged self-administration of drugs which, though initially harmless, leads to complications—sometimes aggravating the condition they were intended to correct. Aspirin, for example, is a medically useful pain-killing (analgesic) drug. An estimated 18 billion aspirin tablets are used each year. But the misuse of aspirin (acetylsalicylic acid) or related substances, particularly among some sensitive individuals, can lead to intestinal bleeding, peptic ulcers, and allergic reaction. (Remember, too, some people can't eat chocolate or strawberries. And unlike, the lady in the hospital mentioned earlier, some individuals drink more than 15 to 18 cups of coffee a day without ill effect).

When taking medicine, you should take the exact doses at the designated times—follow the instructions. The physician or the pharmacist or both should clearly explain the procedures to be followed. If they don't, be sure to ask. Additional precautions are:

- —keep only those medicines being used
- —discard or destroy old medicines (they lose their strength and change chemical composition over time)
- —read the labels carefully, under good reading conditions
- —when taking more than one medicine, close the bottle or box of the first before opening the second
- —pour liquids with labels up to keep them clean and readable
- —keep medications in the original container, properly identified
- —don't take medicines in the dark at night; turn on the lights and put on your glasses if necessary
- —don't keep medicines at the bedside; taking medications (by yourself) while sleepy can result in overdosages. (3)

Childhood Poisoning

Poisoning may well be the most common medical hospital emergency among young children (4). Childhood poisonings take about one thousand young lives each year. Freud described this age as the "oral stage." Infants and toddlers explore the world by testing things with their mouths. Almost anything that fits—and some that do not—is licked, tasted, chewed, or swallowed. In a California study, the leading fatal poison for children under five years was aspirin and other salicylates. (5) Petroleum products, usually solvents, and pesticides were next in rank.

Recommendations for the prevention of poisoning include: enforcement of laws requiring labelling of hazardous substances; development and use of safety caps and closed containers; keeping dangerous substances locked away and out of children's reach; and, continuing education of children and the public about the use of hazardous substances. Perhaps the most significant recommendations are related to our attitudes about the carefree ingestion of drugs in later life: par-

ents should administer drugs to children in a matter-of-fact manner—
play no games with medications; and, it might be well for parents
to avoid, whenever possible, taking pills or medicines in the presence
of young children.

The Social Environment

Perhaps because we are a nation of doers, we are impatient. Many
illness and discomforts of nature will pass with time. Even our physicians may have lost sight of the advice of one of the great medical
practitioners, Sir William Osler: "One of the first duties of the physician is to educate the masses not to take medicine." Perhaps we are
spoiled and can't stand discomfort. We demand of our physicians the
latest "wonder drug" publicized in popular magazines. Thus, through
the misuse of penicillin, some of us have developed an allergy and
can no longer use it. A fatal reaction, called anaphylactic shock, is
possible. In addition some of the microorganisms formerly susceptible
to the drug have developed resistance. For example, venereal diseases
once easily cured by penicillin are now more difficult to treat. Furthermore, there are the so-called "side effects" of drugs which are in vary-
ing degrees harmless or merely annoying or possibly harmful. Antihistamines, useful for the reduction of sniffles, sneezing, and the stuffy
nose of hay fever, are also the cause of drowsiness which can be un-
desirable even hazardous.

We seem to have become a society dedicated to avoid discomfort
and tension. Advertising on radio, television, and in magazines sells
us pills for our livers, stomachs, and bowels; salves for skin and hemor-
rhoids; washes for our mouths and eyes; and more pills and tablets to
help us relax, "reduce tension" and sleep. These are the nonprescription
drugs—proprietary drugs—purchased over-the-counter. There are an estimated one billion prescriptions for "ethical" drugs written each year.
Comedians have tired of chiding us as a pill-taking generation; we
take pills to wake up—to go to sleep; to be calm—to be stimulated; to
lose weight—to gain weight; to promote conception—to prevent conception; and soon we will have pills to help us remember after taking pills
to help us forget. To argue whether Madison Avenue drug advertising
causes us to use drugs or we want them and thus encourage advertising is much like the "chicken and egg" argument.

Drug abuse, in past years, was considered to be a phenomenon of
the city—particularly the inner-city or slum areas. Crime, juvenile de-
linquency, and drug abuse are associated with poverty, deprivation,
broken homes, lack of parental supervision, insecurity, lack of opportunity for creative or productive activity, and boredom. In the suburbs, they are associated with affluence, over-indulgence, permissiveness,
broken homes, lack of parental supervision, insecurity, failure to utilize
opportunities for creative and productive activity and boredom. Though

there are differing socio-economic and cultural aspects of the inner-cities, urban areas, and suburbs which tend to lead to differing abuses, there are notable similarities in drug abuse.

The proximity and number of outlets such as drug stores, doctors' offices, hospitals, laboratories, manufacturing plants, and warehouses may affect the availability of drugs and consequently the number of drug abusers. A 1962 survey by the Food and Drug Administration showed that approximately one million pounds of barbiturates and over one hundred thousand pounds of amphetamines were available in the United States. This represents about 24 doses of the former and up to 50 doses of the latter for every man, woman, and child in the nation. Production in such quantities is testimony to the medical usefulness of these drugs and large quantities are legally prescribed. The expanding variety of these medicines provides the physician with a greater aramentarium for individual patients and particular conditions. Unfortunately, through pilfering, stealing, and even counterfeiting, large quantities are illegally obtained for black market sale. Drugs smuggled into the country add to the problem and are difficult to control especially when they reach the cities.

Many authorities believe that except in order to maintain the drug habit crime is not always an effect of drug abuse—particularly among juveniles. (In November 1969, newspapers reported the arrest of several men in New York City who were bartering with junior high school students who brought them burglarized goods in exchange for drugs.) Crime and drugs are related in the high crime areas of the inner-cities. The Bureau of Narcotics estimated, in 1965, there were sixty thousand "addicts" (primarily dependent upon heroin) in five major cites. (6) Maintaining a "habit" can cost as much as $75 to $100 per day. Fifty per cent of New York City's crimes are attributed to drug "addicts." Estimates of their cost in crime runs as high as ten million dollars a day.

Undoubtedly, there are more arrests for drug violations in the cities than in the suburbs and rural areas combined. Currently, college communities are target areas for drug users and pushers. Conditions are less conducive to detection among other factors. In the last few years, among juveniles, arrests for heroin abuse have decreased while increases occur for such drugs as marihuana, amphetamines, and barbiturates. In Los Angeles, in 1966, two thousand juveniles were arrested for drug violations—in 1967, four thousand. Seventy-four per cent of the arrests were for marihuana. (7) How many unreported drug users and drug dependent persons there are—particularly among college students and those in the middle and upper classes—is open to speculation.

When law enforcement in the control of drugs is effective, types of drug abuse and even drug dependency changes. For example, when large shipments or caches of heroin or marihuana are intercepted and confiscated, drug abusers are likely to either temporarily or permanently change drugs. This may be a factor in multi-habituation. On the other hand, some "druggies" may take the opportunity to "kick the habit."

Deviant Social Behavior

We can observe a variety of acceptable or tolerated behavior in our pluralistic, complex, and industrialized society. Perhaps our tense, frenetic, anxiety-producing way of life leads to the abuse of almost everything including sex, money, tobacco, power, and even freedom. Why do we tolerate some apparent abuses and reject others? We even encourage the use and abuse of alcohol even though there are an estimated 5 to 6 million alcoholics and eleven thousand deaths each year due to acute alcoholism. The comment is made that alcohol "fits" better in our society because in addition to being tension-reducing it facilitates interpersonal relationships. (8) In other societies which have a different value structure and which emphasize the contemplative life, alcohol is feared and other drugs tend to be tolerated. Thus, in a competitive, impersonal, urban society substances or behaviors are suspect which turn people inward on themselves causing them to retreat from socialization into their own private worlds. The history of western man has been accompanied by the use of alcohol and celebrated in the cup. Eastern cultures have not widely adopted alcohol. Most of their religions expressly forbid it.

Who can say with certainty why we classify the use of some drugs as criminal behavior while other drugs with similar "mind-manifesting" effects are acceptable? It seems that in our society drug use for only therapeutic purposes is sanctioned. Except for alcohol, coffee (caffeine) and tobacco, drug use to enhance mental-emotional patterns is considered deviant. As with the confusion between the definitions of addiction and habituation, the criteria for establishing drug abuse and deviant behavior are—the law notwithstanding—difficult to specify.

The norms or standards of behavior developed by society, always changing, now seem to be in a state of flux. The do's and don'ts, the should's and should not's, both written and unwritten, secular and religious, are subject to question and scientific scrutiny. That which was once accepted on faith is being tested. New norms or limits have not yet evolved. When once we were concerned with behavioral controls in an environment of scarcity of goods and manpower, we now have abundance and technology. We have the time, energy, and resources to explore and question. Where once we associated only with relatives and lifelong neighbors, we now move about among various racial, ethnic, and religious groups. Exposure to different values leads us to doubt our own. When once we were "destined" to fit into the role expected of us by family and society—to follow our father's occupation, —we now ascribe to achievement in any self-selected, tolerated endeavors. The emphasis on "achieving" seems to have created many psychological and social pressures. The failure rate in terms of individuals who can't (or who are afraid to try) make it in our society has risen steadily.

1. Can you recall how many "medicines" you prescribed for yourself in the past 60 days? Take a survey in class to establish the total and an average.
2. Are there any "medicines" handed-down from your grandparents that are still being used in your family? What are they? What are they used for? Are they effective?
3. Can you recall in your reading of history or literature the incidents in which medicines or drugs or alcohol played a significant part?
4. How many famous people—past or present—can you identify who were known drug-users or alcoholics? What were the consequences?
5. Is there a Poison Center in your area? What is it? How does it function?

War, atomic bombs, hypocrisy, the generation gap, and a host of other social phenomena needing sound thinking, have been listed by young people as reasons to "tune out and turn on" with . . . whatever drug is available and fashionable. Is it a "cop out"?

REFERENCES
1. LASAGNA, LOUIS, M.D., "Drugs Through the Ages," in *The Medicated Society,* edited by Samuel Proger, M.D., New York: The Macmillan Company, 1968, p. 7.
2. Food and Drug Administration, *The Use and Misuse of Drugs,* Publication No. 46, Washington, D. C.: U.S. Government Printing Office, 1968, p. 6.
3. Adapted from: American Medical Association, *Medicines and How to Use Them.* MD—Patient Information Service Pamphlet, Chicago, Illinois, 1964.
4. ARENA, JAY, M., M.D., "Poisonings Have Many Names," *Hospital Tribune,* March 10, 1969, p. 5.
5. WEST, IRMA, M.D., "Fatal Accidental Poisonings: Patterns Revealed," *California's Health,* 22:169-171, March 15, 1965.
6. National Institute of Mental Health, *Facts About Narcotic Drug Addiction,* Public Health Service Publication No. 1322, Washington, D. C.: U.S. Government Printing Office, 1965, p. 2.
7. CWALINA, GUSTAV E., "Drug Use on High School and College Campuses," *Journal of School Health,* 38:638-646, December, 1968.
8. DINITZ, SIMON, DYNES, RUSSELL R., and CLARKE, ALFRED C., *Deviance,* New York: Oxford University Press, 1969, p. 277.

CHAPTER 3

The Drug User

That everyone is a drug user should now be apparent. But not everyone is a drug abuser. Most, it appears use drugs properly—only when necessary, according to instructions, and under medical supervision. Others are "hooked" on proprietary drugs—over-the-counter items —such as laxatives or cathartics, gas-reducers (bromides), tonics and cough medicines, relaxants, stay-awakes, and pain-killers (analgesics). Still others seem to be compelled to abuse more potent, more toxic, more dangerous substances.

In our "go-go" highly competitive society, pressure and emotional manifestations can be associated with the excessive use of and dependence upon coffee, alcohol, tobacco, food, sex, work, money, power, and, of course, drugs. Who is the drug abuser? Who will become drug dependent? The harried or over-weight housewife, the intense hard-driving executive, the over-worked physician, the jazz-musician, the immature teen-ager, the anxious college student, the hippy, the curious— anyone, everyone may be eligible.

Most youths in our highly advanced technological and affluent society are relatively assured of security. Survival, in the economic sense, is not a serious question. (However, survival in consideration of atomic and biologic war-fare, and man's pollution of the environment which disrupts ecological systems is something else). The challenge of growing up, becoming and striving is, on the one hand, greatly lessened. On the other, the achievement of the tasks of development— particularly from early adolescence through young adulthood—are harder to accomplish. Proof of masculinity or femininity, independence, skill, power, and courage is more complex and more difficult to demonstrate.

Risk-taking through drag racing or speeding cars, illegal acts, sexually exploitive behavior, and drug taking are some ways young people attempt to develop self-esteem and recognition. For some, even a successful athletic career is not sufficient or daring enough to satisfy emotional needs.

To challenge the "system" or the establishment, some young people have been growing long hair and beards, wearing old clothes, not bathing, living primitively, and using drugs. Some contend the hippy is a manifestation of guilt by young adults who feel they have been given too much without earning it.

Learning to live with affluence may be more difficult than we realize. For us, it seems to have brought a longer period of economic and emotional dependence. The development of maturity is delayed (and, as can be seen in some adults, arrested). A Freudian definition of maturity is the ability to postpone gratification, to tolerate present discomfort or pain in order to achieve a goal and thus greater satisfaction at some later time. The immature demand instant gratification— the pleasure principle. Drug abuse is often looked upon as basically immature behavior.

Categorizing people and things is a favorite pastime for most of us. It is a necessary technique for organizing and ordering knowledge. However, as lazy thinkers, we abuse the use of categories and develop stereotypes. Our efforts should be stronger made to identify and judge individuals, and the following sections are offered with this in mind.

Characteristics of Drug Abusers

The lines are not clear between those habituations and dependencies which we tolerate and those to which we object. But there seems to be a concensus that drug dependency is most often symptomatic of personality maladjustment. Nevertheless, no typical "addict personality" has yet been described. Attempting to do so, one author succeeds in identifying almost everyone:

1. *Normal*—those mentally healthy persons who are accidentally addicted through the use of habit-forming drugs during treatment for an illness.
2. *Psychoneurotics*—hedonistic individuals who seek pleasure, new excitements, and sensations.
3. *Character disorder*—psychoneurotics with mild hysterical symptoms, phobias, compulsions, and other neurotic pathology.
4. *Personality disorder*—habitual criminals, psychopaths with extreme antisocial behavior.
5. *Inadequate or sociopathic personality*—addictive personalities with an ungovernable need for intoxicants. (1)

Though primarily concerned with the abuse of narcotics, the writer has in fact described five psychologic categories which includes potential dependants on any type of drug. In general, it appears, the more severe the emotional disorder, the greater the abuse involving more potent and thus more dangerous drugs.

In an exploratory study of 200 non-institutionalized adults in the San Francisco area, there appears to be some differentiating characteristics among "low drug users" and "high drug users." (2) The former group using only common items such as tobacco, alcohol, aspirin, laxatives, and prescribed pain-killers; the latter using exotic and illicit drugs such as marihuanas, heroin and LSD. A middle group used essentially medically prescribed drugs. The findings suggest that those with greater drug experience will believe in medications and will self-medicate more, enjoy the role of patient, and will have had more medical care.

Psychological conflicts associated with eating problems—orality—are reported more frequently among the more drug experienced. Dislike of parents, especially fathers of illicit-exotic drug users—demonstrating rebellion against authority—is expressed by high drug users. Also, this group is more dissatisfied with themselves, their work, and relations with others. Cravings, unsatisfied desires, extreme likes and dislikes, and drug-dependency fears characterize the high drug user. They more often tried drugs on a "dare" when young. They report their drug use is for religious and self-analytical purposes or as a matter of curiosity and experimentation.

The high drug users also reported more accidental overdoses and the use of drugs for suicide attempts. Background differences from low to high drug use show increases in education, divorce, youth, and the number of whites. Church affiliations, age, and the number of Negroes and Orientals increase as the drug experience goes from high to low. Other characteristics lead the researcher to the generalization, "Perhaps 'conservatives' comes close for the least-drug-experience people, 'middle class' for the high normals, and 'liberal disaffiliated' for the illicit-exotic people." (3)

A psychiatrist exploring the motivation of intelligent young drug takers identifies three broad groups: the experience seekers, the oblivion seekers, and the personality-change seekers. (4) The first are experimenters, many of whom are rebellious or hostile, and wish to break the rules.

The oblivion-seekers find the drugged state of mind is pleasant—an escape from worldly stresses. They claim disgust with the hypocrisy, materialism, and competitiveness of the older generation. Some are burdened by feelings of incompetence and inadequacy. Some feel "trapped" in the restrictive higher education process. Some are depressed and take greater risks with drugs sometimes leading to fatal overdoses.

The personality-change seekers are those who most often become drug dependent or permanently incapacitated by drugs. Frustration and disappointment lead to larger doses and use of drugs in combinations. Many are psychologically disturbed—severe neurotics, schizophrenics, manic-depressives, and psychopaths. Some are disturbed about their sexuality. Some are alienated, unmotivated, and lonely and seek solace and companionship in the drug using group. A few hope that drug experience will change them, others expect drug taking will help them make friends and enhance communication.

Youth and Drugs in the Cities

Youthful and young adult drug takers are frequently associated with gangs and the "street society." (5) Drug problems more readily develop in an environment which brings together emotionally or psychologically disturbed persons and available supplies of drugs. Under the intense conditions of the inner-city environment, youthful experimentation with "soft" drugs is short-lived or by-passed and progress to the "hard" stuff, narcotics, occurs more rapidly. (The terms "hard" and "soft" are street vernacular used to distinguish between narcotics, known to produce physical dependence and which involved federal penalties, and non-narcotic drugs for which there were no federal penalties. Another distinguishing characteristic seems to be that "hard" drugs are essentially "body" drugs—affecting physical feelings, while "soft" drugs are essentially "mind" drugs—affecting mental states. Both categories, however, affect the whole person to some extent, and both are dangerous. Revised federal laws include restrictions and penalties for both).

The problem of drug abuse and dependency on dangerous drugs among youth increased first in the cities. The increase from 2000 to 4000 juveniles arrested in one recent year in Los Angeles was cited. In 1964, there were 763 arrests in Chicago for possession of heroin. (6) Eight hundred and eighty-six were arrested for possession of marihuana. Also, among youths 17 to 20 years old, 459 were arrested for possession (use?) of amphetamines and barbiturates. One year later, 1965, arrests showed a decrease to 538 for possession of heroin and an increase to 1321 for marihuana. The Vice Control Division of the Chicago Police Department reported an increase to 549 arrests of 17 to 20 year olds for possession of amphetamines and barbiturates. In New York, police records showed a similar trend among youths moving away from heroin abuse and associated narcotics to amphetamines, barbiturates, and marihuana. Those escaping detection and arrest would increase the numbers many fold. Currently in New York City, an increase in the number of "hard" drug users is evident.

As new youths are "recruited" or exposed to drugs, the preference seems to have been for the easy to obtain, easy to take, mind-affecting drugs with less serious criminal offenses at stake. Actually, the average age of the heroin abuser is several years older than those on "pop" drugs. (More recent reports, at present unconfirmed, indicate an increase of heroin abuse in suburbs and near college campuses. This could indicate a reversal of the earlier trend, the dissemination of both types of drugs throughout society, a transition among college age youth to narcotics, or the association of narcotics users with campus communities where drug experimentation and use can be exploited for profit.)

Developmental, psychological, and environmental problems of youths (perhaps, moreso in the cities) are obvious factors in their decisions to use drugs. The relationship of such problems is reflected in this observation of young institutionalized "addicts":

> The fact that high school graduates were rare among this group, and that most had a history of difficulties with school adjustment which antedates their initial use of drugs, suggested that their deviant behavior patterns were probably established and supported at an early age. (7)

Emotional problems characterize drug dependent youths referred to as "addicts" by earlier researchers. Such characteristics as impulsiveness, low thresholds of frustration, impatience, a sense of immediacy, and fear of failure, particularly in school, have been identified. (8) For some youths matters are more complicated. A study which received national attention indicated that some young "addicts" had passive or dependent fathers and immature mothers who helped to perpetuate the "addiction" in their sons to gratify their own dependent needs. (9) A pre-existing mental or emotional disturbance is frequently associated with drug abuse.

Such factors as associations with drug users, pressure from peers in juvenile groups, curiosity, and thrill-seeking are strongly related to the beginnings of drug abuse. Actually, most new drug takers, particularly in the suburbs and on college campuses, get their first samples from friends and not from professional pushers as is commonly believed. Friends, it seems, want to "share their experience." Or can it be that they want to settle their anxiety by seducing others to convince themselves that drug abuse is all right? Sometimes when the drug habit gets expensive "friends" become pushers. The daily newspapers provide ample evidence of the numerous arrests of "non-criminal, student types" with large quantities of drugs intended for re-sale to "friends." The profit motive more than the drug experience is sometimes the reason for selling drugs among college students and suburban youths as well as to inner-city drug takers.

Drug Users in College

Evidence that use and abuse of drugs on campuses is increasing continues to accumulate. Most users, it must be said, should be classified as experimenters. They do not express a desire to continue non-medical drug use and after two or three episodes will give it up. However, in 1967, on one west coast campus, 21 per cent had tried marihuana with four per cent identifying themselves as regular users. Roughly eighteen months later 57 per cent reported marihuana experience with about 14 per cent claiming regular use. (10) At the same time there was evidence of increased use of other psychoactive drugs.

A correlation between rates of drug use (particularly hallucinogens) and "intellectual climate" is proposed. (11) Drug use is defined as those who "ever tried" drugs for their effect on mood, feeling, or psychological states (psychoactive). Highest rates are associated with small, progressive, liberal arts colleges with high faculty-student ratios, high student ability as measured by College Board examinations, close student-faculty relationships, and great value placed on academic independence, intellectual interests, and personal freedom of students. (The writer does not indicate how these attributes are identified.) At a dozen or so of these institutions the use of hallucinogens is said to exceed 50 per cent of the student body. Lowest rates of drug use—estimated at five per cent or less, rarely more—are to be found in colleges noted for their vocational programs, absence of intellectual interest, and presence of anti-intellectual technical training or social, fraternity, and sports activities sub-groups. Correspondingly, at large universities, drug use would be higher among the colleges of Arts and Sciences, Drama, Music, Literature, Art and Architecture, and Graduate School as compared to Engineering, Education, and Business Administration. In any case, drug use in colleges seems to be exaggerated since there appears to be so little of it on most of the many college campuses. The question is raised, "Do colleges with an "intellectual climate" recruit student types who are drug experimenters or does the climate and culture of the college lead students to use drugs?" To what extent drugs are used symbolically—as an artifact of the intellectual or creative person—or as a true attempt at "insights" is not established. Claims that drugs enhance learning and creativity are not proven and may be rationalizations.

The popular version of the young adult drug taker is that of a hedonistic or pleasure-seeking, hippie-type, irresponsible, and spoiled wastrel. The adjectives—or epithets—used to describe the "druggies" are also used for college student drug users. The association of non-students, or ex-students, with those on the campuses tends to reinforce this image in the public eye. Frequently, drug users—particularly experimenters—are those students with better than average grades. Nevertheless, the distinction between the groups is not readily apparent since many drug users are college drop-outs. Also, it seems that among those drop-outs who are not psychologically disturbed, many return to finish school within a few years.

The reasons for using drugs given by students are similar to those of non-students: curiosity; getting "high"; exploring the mind and self; experiencing religious or spiritual insights; reducing boredom; overcoming fear or depression; relaxing from pressures; enhancing sexual experience; reducing sexual tensions; and escape from a hostile world. Sometimes students indicate they use drugs to help them study. Sometimes they indicated drugs were used for an attempt at suicide.

Students who use hallucinogens, marihuana, and opiates (only a small but increasing percentage use opiates) have been characterized as: older upperclassmen, in arts-humanities or social sciences, from wealthy families, in opposition to parental values, political activists, left-wing, irreligious, dissatisfied, pessimistic, heavy users of mild stimulants, and have had drop-out experiences. (12)

Categorizing drug abusers by social class, education, or race is tenuous if not impossible. More and more drug users and drug dependent individuals are found among almost all groups. The Bureau of Narcotics and Dangerous Drugs in the U.S. Department of Justice considers three main groups. The "situational" user takes drugs for a purpose: weight-control pills for energy to finish household chores; and, amphetamines to stay awake for studying or for overnight motor trips. Psychological dependence may or may not be present.

The second group, usually of high school or college age, are "spree" users—for "kicks" or "experience" or sometimes in defiance of convention. They usually take drugs in social situations. There may be some degree of psychological dependence exhibited but because of sporadic and mixed pattern of use, little or no physical dependence.

The "hard-core" drug abuser or "addict" comprises the last group. He (usually males) has a strong psychological dependence, and depending upon the drug of choice, often is physically dependent. His life-style consists largely of activities involved with obtaining and using drugs. He feels he cannot function without the support of drugs. Generally, the hard-core abuser suffers from some emotional or psychiatric disorder—either not apparent or not diagnosed—before his initial drug abuse experience.

Many, if not most "addicts" have their first drug experience in adolescence. Many young people have emotional difficulties facing the loosening of family ties, reduction of parental authority, sexual maturation, and increasing responsibilities. Anxious, frustrated, fearing failure, and full of doubts and inner conflicts, the immature adolescent may use drugs to loosen inhibitions, find companionship, heighten sensations, or to provide relief and escape.

There is much overlap between the situational, spree, and hard-core drug users. For some, a transition to the hard-core group occurs when personality and the effects of drugs leads to a loss of control over the use of drugs. Currently, there is controversy over the use of "harmless" drugs (i.e., marihuana) by fairly large numbers of people. Not considering themselves emotionally unstable, they feel free to use such drugs as they chose and wish legal restrictions to be removed.

In the chapters that follow on the types of drugs, additional information on the social and psychological factors will provide a wider perspective of drug abuse. However, honesty compels this writer to point out that absolutely true facts regarding drugs are difficult to come by. Even scientists, as well as science-minded people, tend to discuss drugs in terms of the natural biases of society. Much research has yet to be done and the ability to present the findings in a completely objective and dispassionate manner is difficult to develop—even in basic pharmacologic texts and journals.

1. Are the psychological characteristics of drug users associated with the "reasons" discussed in Chapter II? How?
2. Which seems to come first—drug abuse or dropping out of school? Can you support your position with evidence?
3. Are drugs abused in your school? Which ones? From whom are they obtained? Can you estimate the incidence or percentage of abusers?
4. From the text, does it appear that a "drug-type" can be described? Is there a characteristic upon which most would agree?
5. Can you or would you place yourself in one of the categories discussed? Which one(s)?
6. Is it possible to identify someone near you as a drug abuser? What are your criteria for doing so?

REFERENCES

1. KOLB, LAWRENCE, *Drug Addiction*, Springfield, Illinois: Charles C. Thomas, Publisher, 1962, p. 38.
2. BLUM, RICHARD H., *Society and Drugs: Drugs I*, Jossey-Bass, Inc., Publishers, 1969, pp. 245-275.
3. *Ibid.*, p. 275.
4. BLAINE, GRAHAM B. JR., M.D., "Why Intelligent Young People Take Drugs," *Journal Iowa State Medical Society*, 59:37-42, January, 1969.
5. WEECH, ALEXANDER A., "The Narcotic Addict and 'The Street'," *Archives of General Psychiatry*, 14:299-306, March, 1966.
6. Personal correspondence and "Excerpts from the Annual Narcotic Report for the Year 1965," Lt. Thomas Kernan, Commanding Officer, Narcotic Section, Chicago Department of Police, Chicago, Illinois.
7. PATRICK, SHERMAN W., "Institutional Treatment of the Juvenile Narcotics User," *Drug Addiction in Youth*, edited by Ernest Harms, New York: Pergamon Press, 1965, p. 10.
8. LASKOWITZ, DAVID, "Psychological Characteristics of the Adolescent Addict," *Drug Addiction in Youth*, edited by Ernest Harms, New York: Pergamon Press, 1965, p. 67.
9. New York Times, "Mothers of Addicts Said to Balk Cures," May 10, 1965, p. 1.
10. BLUM, RICHARD H., *Students and Drugs: Drugs II*, Jossey-Bass, Inc., Publishers, 1969, p. 191.
11. KENISTON, KENNETH, "Heads and Seekers: Drugs on Campus, Counter-Cultures, and American Society," *The American Scholar*, Winter, 1968, pp. 97-112.
12. BLUM, *op. cit.*, p. 142.

CHAPTER 4

Glue-Sniffing

Glue-sniffing is a term which now represents the inhalation of many volatile substances for the purpose of experiencing their intoxicating or euphoric effects. Youngsters and adults have practiced inhaling gasoline, cleaning fluid, paint thinner, finger-nail polish remover, lighter fluids, and a variety of volatile hydrocarbons. The incidence of abuse has increased in recent years particularly among youngsters 8 to 18 years of age. (In Japan, it is a fairly widespread practice among young adults).

Model airplane glue has been most widely abused in recent years. Polystyrene cement is inexpensive, easy to purchase, easy to steal, easy to conceal, and, heretofore, a commonly accepted household product. Through rapid evaporation—made more intense by heat—the sniffer inhales the constituent compounds such as toluene, benzene, chloroform, and alcohol. (In the early days after the development of ether, young medical students were known to inhale enough to experience ether "jags"). Frequently, the glue is spread on a cloth or handkerchief which is held to the mouth and nose and sniffed. Thus sniffing sometimes takes place in full view of unsuspecting parents or teachers—particularly if the subject pretends to be yawning or sneezing. Sometimes the glue is squeezed into a plastic bag which is then held to the face— or more dangerously placed over the head—for inhalation.

For gasoline and other liquids, sniffing is often accomplished directly from the can or bottle. Painters and workers in factories where such products are used will often experience a form of intoxication if ventilation is inefficient.

General Effects of Glue-Sniffing

The sniffer will probably exhibit the same behavior as in the first stages of alcohol intoxication. In the first half hour or so, blurring of vision, ringing in the ears, loss of coordination, slurring of speech, and perhaps hallucinations will occur. Drunkenness is the typical symp-

20

tom. A sense of floating or spinning is often experienced. Marked changes of mood can occur. After this follows a let-down period. Drowsiness, stupor, perhaps nausea, and sometimes unconsciousness are exhibited. This period is frequently blanked-out to memory after recovery.

Hazards of Glue-Sniffing

Immediate hazards are essentially behavioral. There are individual differences in behavior among glue sniffers (as with many drug-abusers). The typical sniffer tends to withdraw into a fantasy-dream world— at least, in most instances. However, sometimes aggressive impulses are released (a characteristic similar to alcohol abuse). Though not common, fights, stabbings, and behavior associated with delusions of grandeur and overpowering strength have occurred. As with some LSD users, believing they could fly or stop trains, sniffers have suffered severe injuries.

Psychological effects are related to detrimental emotional health. Mild or temporary dependence on glue-sniffing is associated with loss of motivation, moodiness, restlessness, and rejection of responsibility. In the more heavily dependent, truancy, dropping-out of school, and law violations are more common. The development of psychological dependence (but no physical dependence) is a significant hazard.

The physical hazards are less clear but significant. The accidental inhalation of the fluid form of volatile substances can be extremely damaging to the lungs, even fatal. In Columbus, Ohio, a ten year old was found dead between two parked cars. The gasoline cap had been removed from the tank nearest the corpse. There were no apparent physical injuries. (Gasoline sniffers tend to operate alone while glue-sniffers tend to operate in groups).

There is evidence of the toxic effect of glue-sniffing on the brain, kidneys, liver, and bone marrow. (1) Alteration or breaks in the chromosomes—the genetic bodies in the cell responsible for hereditary traits —as well as liver damage have been reported. (2) Newspapers reported, in March, 1969, 100 paint thinner deaths in Japan during the 1968 year.

Discussion

Eradication of sniffing behavior is undoubtedly impossible. Only a remarkable change in the psycho-social environment and in the emotional health of those who would abuse drugs and inhale solvents will effect a reduction. Though dangerous in itself, authorities are concerned with the progress of young abusers to other hazardous and illegal drugs. To reduce glue-sniffing, at least one manufacturer will be adding oil of mustard to plastic model cements. Working with the substance is no problem but attempting to sniff the vapors is extremely uncomfortable. This still leaves a wide variety of volatile substances which can be abused.

1. Do you like the smell of gasoline? How many of you purposely inhale in the presence of gasoline? Would you consider this abuse?
2. Why do you suppose anyone would want to continuously inhale the vapors of glue?
3. Have you ever experienced a "jag" (intoxicating effects) while using or in the presence of house paint or cleaning fluid? Can you describe the sensations?
4. If there were no physical damage would glue-sniffing still be hazardous? How?
5. Do you know of a glue-sniffing case? Have you read about one? Discuss the characteristics.

In Columbus, Ohio, a tragic story was unfolded in the death of an 18-year-old boy who died as a consequence of inhaling vegetable oil spray from an aerosol can. (3) Parental conflict, misunderstanding, lack of constructive activities and pressures from peers in school—even in a loving and caring family—are parts of the story. A similar incident was reported in a Washington, D. C. suburb. (4) Perhaps there was a tragedy like these in your hometown.

REFERENCES
1. CORLISS, LELAND, M.D., "A Review of the Evidence on Glue-Sniffing—A Persistent Problem," *Journal of School Health*, 35:442-449, December, 1965.
2. Medical News, "Glue Sniffing May Alter Chromosomes: Other Solvents Also Implicated," *Journal of the American Medical Association*, 207:1441-1442, 1448, February 24, 1969.
3. GARRETT, BETTY, "Boy Tried to Cite Problem, Dad Recalls," *Columbus Citizen-Journal*, January 9, 1969, pp. 1, 2.
4. KLOSE, KEVIN, "Youth, 15, Was 'A Victim of the Times'," *Washington Post*, May 17, 1969, pp. 1, A9.

CHAPTER 5

Hallucinogens

Many natural hallucinogenic drugs have been used in various so-cieties throughout history. There seems to be about forty known plant-derived hallucinogens in the Western Hemisphere. These were used mostly in mystical-religious ceremonies. Though some are still used this way by southwestern Indians, many are being abused in our college population.

Of the drugs classified in this category, most produce similar re-actions though of different intensities. The differences are due to the manner in which each affects the central nervous system and their vary-ing potencies. True hallucinations, as an effect, seem to be the ex-ception rather than the rule. Nevertheless, they are often used inter-changeably or in combinations. Depending upon many conditions, including the attitude and expectations (mind-set) of the user, these drugs are considered to be: psychotomimetic—seeming to mimic psy-choses or mental disorders; psychotogenic—producing a state of psy-choses; psychedelic or psychodelic, also known as "mind-manifesting"—characterized by enjoyable perceptual changes and highly creative thought patterns; and, hallucinogenic—producing hallucinations which are sense perceptions not founded in objective reality. Usually, a user under the influence of the drug can distinguish between reality and his visions or mental images. This would not be considered a true hallucination.

Commonly identified in this group are LSD-25 (d-lysergic acid diethylamide tartarate), psilocybin and psilocin (extracts of the "Magic Mushroom" Psylocybe mexicana and stropharia cubensis), peyote and mescaline (from the Mexican peyotl cactus buttons which grow above ground), and DMT (dimethyltryptamine also known as parica which is found in the cahobe bean of South America). Others in this group are ololuiqui seeds (from a tropical morning glory), datura strammo-nium or Jimson weed, mandrake, nutmeg, and even catnip (Nepeta cataria) and morning glory seeds (Ipomoea). More recent additions, not found in nature but synthesized in the laboratory, are DOM, popularly known as STP (4-methyl-2, 5 dimethoxamphetamine) and DET (diethyltryptamine).

Some drugs to be discussed in other categories sometimes have hallucinogenic effects. Since these are secondary effects, these drugs are not included here. Marihuana, however, though legally classified with the narcotics is best considered with the hallucinogens. (By the time you read this booklet the Federal laws on marihuana may have been revised.)

Hallucinogens have no medical uses though experimentation by authorized researchers continues. To use (abuse) these drugs one must obtain them illegally.

General Patterns of Hallucinogen Abuse

The use of hallucinogens depends upon a number of factors. Knowledge of the effects of drugs will determine the choice. An unpleasant and dangerous drug like datura strammonium is not widely used. Use of LSD on campuses may also be decreasing as knowledge is accumulated and communicated. Availability of drugs and their cost, laws and moral values, group structure and support, effects—satisfactory or unsatisfactory—will determine their continued use.

Three main groups of users have been identified. (1) The first, consists of heavy drug abusers—those primarily dependent upon narcotics. They occasionally use hallucinogens—usually in combination or sequence with their preferred narcotic—for "kicks" or "curiosity." The second group are commonly called the "acidheads" or "potheads"— the marihuana "potheads" are more numerous. The "hippy," the "arty folk," the "nonconformists," the "frustrated," and the "rebellious" are in this group. Week-end parties and "group occasions" find them using hallucinogens for escape, for insight, for sensual experience, for interpersonal relationships, and reduction of inhibitions. The third group are heavy users (abusers) of hallucinogens exclusively. These are fewer in number and who seem to seek mainly an insightful or spiritual experience or a greater sensitivity to nature.

General Effects of Hallucinogens

There are several physical effects of the hallucinogens which vary in intensity from one drug to another or may not appear at all. Dilation of the pupils, increased blood pressure, increased heart rate (tachycardia), increased blood sugar, irregular breathing, chills and flushes, trembling of the extremities, restlessness, sleeplessness, nausea, headache, dry mouth and severe thirst are among the physical reactions. A period of thirty to forty-five minutes may pass, after oral ingestion, before these effects on the sympathetic nerve system appear. The psychotomimetics are notable for the wide variety of effects they produce— many of which are disagreeable. (2)

As mentioned earlier, the conditions in which these drugs are used will help to determine their effects: potency of the dosage; expectations and personality of the user; the social setting and the psychological context in which use occurs; and the users physical condition. (3) The subjective effects are the main reason for abuse and perhaps the main source of hazards. These really represent possible effects, since the variation is great, rather than typical reactions.

Sense perceptions are distorted even at relatively small dosages. The perception of light and space is affected. Colors seem especially bright and seem to glow. Space between objects becomes more apparent; cracks and irregularities stand out. Objects seem to move and change size, lines may seem wavy; and geometric patterns may appear. One's proprioceptive sense is distorted so that the body may seem to change size and the extremities appear out of proportion.

Particularly with heavier doses, hallucinatory reactions of greater intensity appear. These are mostly visual and the experience (usually with LSD) is intensifed by synesthesia—transposing sensual experiences. A user may report he "hears" colors, "sees" sounds, and "feels" light or music. Since the user can usually continue to distinguish these reactions as subjective and due to the effects of the drug, they are pseudo-hallucinations.

The unpredicability of the hallucinogens is the greatest danger. Swings in moods and emotions occur. Sometimes opposing emotions are sensed simultaneously. Blackness, ugly colors gloom, and isolation are occasionally perceived. Panic, withdrawal, and attempts at violence have occurred. Unpleasant perceptions of one's own body, a distortion of facial expressions (in a mirror or in the imagination), and a "decaying" of the flesh may be experienced. While still the exception rather than the rule, fear, depression, and psychotic states requiring extensive mental therapy may persist long after the experience. The loss of the boundaries of self-identity—knowing one's "inside" from what is "outside"—causes a paranoic state. Internal impulses are externalized and the paranoiac accuses "others" of these impulses. Some users believe they have become omnipotent and have tried to fly from rooftops and windows or tried to stop onrushing traffic and trains.

When the more favorable experiences are encountered, one has had a "good trip." Bad trips are known as "bum trips" or "bummers." These are expressions most common to the "acidheads" or users of LSD and mescaline. Users of hallucinogens—particularly LSD—take "trips" in the presence of a non-user who can act as a guide ("co-pilot" or "conductor") to prevent (if possible) irrational behavior and to help maintain contact with reality.

Some believe hallucinogens are aphrodisiacs—drugs that arouse the sexual instinct. Others claim their sexual potency is reduced. Hallucinogens actually seem to have no effect on the sexual drive. However, if the user has sex in mind, sexual performance is possible and claims of extended sensuality are reported. Generally, the drug user is pre-occupied with the psychological and subjective experience and does not seek a sexual partner.

Continued use of the hallucinogens is associated with the development of psychological dependence. Fortunately, physiological dependence has not yet been demonstrated. Other hazards will be mentioned in the brief discussions of a few of the more commonly abused hallucinogens. Though marihuana is more widely abused, LSD is considered first since it is, at present, more dangerous.

LSD-25

Lysergic acid diethylamide tartarate is a man-made derivative of ergot—a fungus that grows as a rust on rye. Synthesized in 1938 in Switzerland by Stoll and Hofman, five years lapsed before Hofman—working on a cure for migraine headaches—discovered its hallucinogenic properties. On the street, LSD is also known as "acid," "Hawk" and "Big Chief" and its users are known as "acidheads." Black marketeers have also used special brand names for their LSD products—"White Lightning," "Blue Dots," "Purple Wedges" and "Yellow Caps," among many others. (4)

Though used experimentally in the treatment of alcoholism and mental illness, there is no currently approved therapeutic use for LSD. It is synthesized illegally from the ergot fungus in deep fermentation processes with suitable equipment. (5) Properly prepared, a single ounce is enough to provide three hundred thousand doses!

Odorless, colorless, and tasteless, LSD is prepared in liquid or crystalline form. A speck of a dose—50 to 200 micrograms—on a sugar cube, cookie, or licked off the back of a stamp can send a user on an 8 to 12 hour "trip." The general effects have been described in the preceding section. (Imagine the reaction of an unsuspecting victim of a "practical joke" in which LSD is given in a cookie, dropped into a punch bowl, or soaked into a cigarette!)

LSD and Creativity

Many users contend that LSD will help them to profound insights and enhanced creativity in art and music. There is no evidence that this is so. Under, the influence of LSD, users can use logic in a limited manner and their "mystical" experiences cannot be explained to others. Art work attempted at these times is of an inferior quality sometimes representative of emotional states. Standard tests for memory show a definite decrease except in a test for digit-recall ability. (3)

Hazards of LSD Abuse

Users, under "proper" conditions, most frequently report "good trips." However, the really experienced users will admit they can never tell when a "bummer" is coming up and how or if they will be able to handle it. Some—probably those with psychological difficulties—have a "bad trip" the very first time.

The most common "bad trip" is associated with panic—an anxiety reaction. The user is frightened because he cannot stop the drug's action and he fears he is losing his mind. Panic reactions are known as "freak outs." A major break with reality due to toxic psychosis induced by the drug includes paranoia. This feeling may last for a few days after the other drug effects have worn off. The user may attempt violence toward others; show extremely poor judgement and attempt to fly out of windows; and, show bizarre even suicidal behaviors related to mind-body dissociation.

Recurrence or "flashback" is a relatively rare but serious reaction. For as long as six months after the ingestion of LSD, the user may experience an acute reaction like the earlier one. Fear of insanity, panic reactions, and long-term depressions occur. A recent case involved the daughter of the well-known television and radio personality, Art Linkletter. His daughter leaped to her death from a window under the effects of a prior experiment with LSD. Though recurrences are more common among frequent users they also tend to occur among those who have had adverse reactions.

Since these drugs are illegal, black marketeers are known to produce inferior even contaminated products in order to make more money. High dosages—900 to 1200 micrograms, also known as "mics"—are claimed, but actually 100 to 200 micrograms, or less, may be present. Sometimes the LSD is contaminated with methamphetamine or "speed" which is more likely to cause a "bad trip." Other combinations, such as methedrine—belladonna—mescaline have been passed off as LSD and caused untoward reactions.

Brain-damage to LSD users has been claimed but is not proven. This claim may be associated with the observation that many "acid-heads" degenerate behaviorally. They lose ambition, lack motivation, drop-out of the main stream of activity, and seem unable to make a comeback. This observation has been noted by several authorities but was particularly emphasized to the author by Allan Y. Cohen, psychologist and former hallucinogen abuser and follower of the notorious Timothy Leary.

Chromosomal damage is reported and also refuted. At present, it is unclear whether or not LSD causes a significant amount of lasting breaks in the genetic material. Other factors related to the drug abuser —other drugs, nutrition, and so on, may confound the results of studies. However evidence indicates that this hazard is a strong possibility.

Perhaps more significant are the possible teratogenic effects being reported. Babies with defects are born to mothers who have taken LSD during their pregnancy (or defective embryos are found after therapeutic and spontaneous abortions) (6) (7). A high incidence of chromosomal breakage was reported in both embryos and mothers. Animal experiments—where dosages are really high—are also cited as evidence. However, no conclusions have yet been reached. Thus far the psychological hazards have been the greatest concern of both users and authorities. The number of "acidheads" appears to be decreasing though its use will no doubt persist.

Marihuana

Currently considered the most widely experimented with and used illegal drug among youth and young adults, marihuana appears to have been increasing in popularity in the upper-middle classes. (8) Otherwise spelled marijuana, it is also known by such names as "pot," "grass," "tea," "weed," "hay," "Indian hay," "Maryjane," "sticks," "joints," "reefers," "roaches," "muggles," and "Acapulco Gold." India and what has been known as Asia Minor appear to be the original source of the hemp plant cannabis sativa L. (Linn) sometimes referred to as cannabis sativa indica. In the Western Hemisphere the plant is known as marihuana. The fibers of the plant were used to make rope, twine, clothing, and paper. The flowering tops and leaves of the female cannabis are used for the intoxicant effects. The seeds were used as bird food (Oh, how the canaries sang!).

In India and Central Asia, raw resin extracted from the tops is called Charas and is smoked or eaten. Cigarettes made of tops is known as Ganja. The leaves, when powdered and mixed with spices, honey, and water, are eaten and drunk and are known as Bhang. In Tunis, Algeria, and Morocco dried crushed tops are smoked as Kif or Takrouri. In Egypt, Greece, Arabia, and Iran, raw resin extract is known as Hashish. (Bhang and hashish are mentioned frequently in the *Arabian Nights*). Asian cannabis, due to soil, climactic conditions, and careful cultivation, is more potent than western cannabis—marihuana. (9)

The history of marihuana goes back thousands of years. Often used with wine, tobacco, opium, and other drugs, marihuana has been used in religious rites and celebrations. Though it has become illegal in most civilized countries, marihuana represents a cash crop to smugglers in many of the eastern nations. In the United States, it is found as a weed or is illicitly cultivated. A significant source is Mexico where it is grown in remote areas and hidden among regular crops such as corn (marihuana grows from four to ten feet high). Long ago it was used as a medicine and to relieve pain during surgery. After the turn of the century, in the U.S., it was used as an analgesic (pain-reliever) and poultice to remove corns. Today there is no known acceptable medical use for marihuana or its derivatives.

The relatively recent discovery of the active chemicals of marihuana known as cannabinols—particularly the tetrahydrocannabinols—may enable the disclosure of more reliable information on both the short and long-range effects of marihuana. Natural and synthetic tetrahydrocannabinols are enabling researchers to experiment with controlled dosages of these psychoactive drugs. Possibly, with new biochemical techniques and carefully controlled experiments, some beneficial uses—hoped for sporadically throughout history—may be discovered. With such an extensive history of experience, it is strange that we are only now beginning to assemble reliable information on what is probably the world's most used psychoactive drug except for alcohol. Consider what is known thus far.

General Effects of Marihuana

Marihuana is usually smoked in cigarettes, pipes, or waterpipes (nargilehs) and sometimes eaten in cookies or candies or drunk in tea. Mostly marihuana is smoked in groups—"Pot parties"—rather than alone. This has an effect on the expected results.

"Joints" or "reefers" contain the mixture of crushed dried leaves, flowers, small twigs and seeds of marihuana and are rolled in paper twisted at the ends to prevent loss. They are thinner and more uneven than tobacco cigarettes. The smoke is inhaled and held in the lungs for as long as possible. Hashish—the resin extract with the higher concentration of tetrahydrocannabinols—is used in a pipe or by placing small pieces on a lit cigarette and inhaling the smoke through a straw. The effects are felt more quickly and more intensely.

Through smoking, the effects are felt within about 15 minutes and may last from 2 to 12 hours. Marihuana enters the bloodstream through the lungs and influences the brain and nervous system. Pharmacologically its action on nerve cells is unclear. With few exceptions—and with variations among individuals—its effects are not unlike those described for hallucinogens generally (also depending upon the conditions of use).

An increase in pulse rate, rise in blood pressure and blood sugar, dilation of pupils, reddening of the eyes, and lowering of body temperature are early physical signs. Also dryness and irritation of mouth and throat (mucuous membranes and bronchial tubes) are experienced. Increased appetite and thirst and sometimes nausea, vomiting, and diarrhea are present. Some loss of physical coordination is another early effect.

The psychoactive effects vary but generally include swings in mood from exhilaration to depression, feelings of contentment and euphoria and of floating above reality and disconnected ideas. This form of intoxication is accompanied by distortions of space and time. Confusion and irritability, sometimes increased motor activity, and poor judgement and loss of memory occur. Usually the user of marihuana is passive, or lethargic, sometimes inhibitions are reduced and repressed anger is expressed. Under high dosages hallucinatory effects like that of LSD are experienced.

Marihuana Plant

Marihuana—flowering tops and leaves

Marihuana leaves

Marihuana—varied packages

Marihuana—course and fine: prepared for cigarettes

Marihuana and Creativity

Coleridge espoused the virtues of marihuana as enhancing his creative ideas for writing. Jazz musicians believed they played better and faster under the influence of marihuana because it "slowed the time" (rhythm). Artists have claimed more creative works as a result of marihuana use. There is no evidence that these claims are true. Only the users "feel" that they are more creative, observers of their output do not agree. A once great jazz drummer, Gene Krupa, admitted after comparing his recordings, he played poorly under the influence of marihuana.

Hazards of Marihuana Abuse

The dangers of marihuana abuse are unclear. As aforementioned, studies with controlled doses of tetrahydrocannabinols are now being done. Reports from Asian countries indicate that its chronic use leads to toxic psychoses and lethargic, nonproductive, behavior. With large doses, particularly "hash," the hallucinatory distortion of body image and depersonalization can be frightening and lead to panic. In some persons, small doses have caused psychotic—paranoiac—reactions and unconventional behavior. Certainly, driving an automobile or operating heavy machinery while intoxicated with marihuana is dangerous. Records do not show fatalities as a result of marihuana abuse. Thus far, no physical dependence is developed but psychological dependence on marihuana seems to be increasing in our population. Psychological dependence in chronic users and psychotic reactions are associated with underlying personality problems and severe neurotic conflicts.

A major part of the difficulty in evaluating the effects of marihuana is the variability of its potency. "Acapulco Gold" is desired over the "pot" grown in the U.S. "Hash" is more potent but charas—not readily available here—is many times more potent than local marihuana. Since it is illegal, dealers often dilute the material or promise "Gold" when they supply "weed." The user is misled in judging the "mildness" of marihuana.

Currently, illegal tetrahydrocannabinol (THC) is marketed. But synthetic THC is expensive and difficult to produce. Represented as THC are mixtures of talcum powder and amphetamines or a minute quantity of THC and tranquilizer. The price per capsule is high and trips are poor or down right bad. (10)

Other Hallucinogens

Mescaline and *Peyote*, also known as "Mesc" and "Big Chief," is used by Indians of the Native American Church by permission of Federal Law. Isolated in 1898 from the peyote cactus plant, mescaline is one of the alkaloids illicitly marketed as a crystalline powder which can be dissolved in water or prepared in gelatin capsules. Mostly swallowed, reports of "skin-popping" (injecting it under the skin-subcutaneously or intramuscularly) or "sniffing" mescaline have appeared. *Peyote* is made of the buttons of the cactus plant sometimes ground-up and placed in gelatin capsules or rolled into little balls. It is known as "buttons," "tops," "moon," "cactus," "bad seed," and "P." A dose of 350 to 500 milligrams of mescaline can produce illusions and hallucinations from 5 to 12 hours. Neither mescaline or peyote appear to produce physical dependence but may produce psychological dependence.

Psilocybin and *Psilocin* are obtained from mushrooms ("Magic Mushrooms") generally grown in Mexico. These too have been used for centuries in Indian rites. It is illegally available in either crystalline, powdered, or liquid form and has effects similar to mescaline but with doses of only 4 to 8 milligrams. Users have been known to develop a tolerance to psilocybin and psilocin but no physical dependence is produced.

Dimethyltryptamine (DMT) is a short-acting hallucinogen. Its effects last about 45 minutes and it is facetiously called "the business man's special." The powdered seeds of plants native to the Carribean area have been used as snuff—known as "cohoba"—in religious ceremonies. Synthetic DMT is illegally marketed. Its vapors are inhaled from smoke given off by burning the ground seeds or powder mixed with tobacco, parsley leaves, or marihuana. Sometimes it is injected. A dose of 60 to 150 milligrams produces hallucinations. No physical dependence but psychological dependence may be caused.

Diethyltryptamine (DET) is related to DMT but is only produced in the laboratory. Usually it is taken by smoking in a mixture of tobacco, tea, parsley, or marihuana. An injection of 50 to 60 milligrams produces visual distortions, dizziness, and a vague sense of time. No information is yet available on its dependency characteristics.

Dimethoxamphetamine (DOM or STP) is not found in nature but is synthesized in the laboratory. Stronger than LSD, STP produces euphoria at 1 to 3 milligrams and pronounced hallucinogenic effects lasting 8 to 10 hours at more than three milligrams. It is reported to be 200 times more powerful than mescaline but only one-tenth as potent as LSD. Little is known of its pharmacological or dependency effects.

The comparative strengths of hallucinogens have been approximated: (12)

Marihuana (swallowed)	30,000	mg.	Mescaline	400	mg.
Peyote buttons	30,000	mg.	Psilocybin	12	mg.
Nutmeg	20,000	mg.	STP	5	mg.
Hashish	4,000	mg.	LSD	0.1	mg.

Discussion

Though conclusive scientific evidence on the hazards of hallucinogens is not yet available, enough is known to affect the disposition to abuse these drugs. LSD is apparently losing its "glamor" as reports of its possible effects on chromosomes and on birth defects are made known. Perhaps only the naive will become experimenters and the alienated-rebellious types the hard users.

Interestingly, reports of widespread use of "acid" and "pot" among younger homosexuals have been noted. Under the influence they seem to feel "liberated" and differentiate themselves from older homosexuals who continue to prefer alcohol for their "kicks."

Marihuana poses greater difficulties in decision-making. True, for most users it appears to be a mild intoxicant. Perhaps it has advantages over alcohol. But to compare mild forms of marihuana with heavy doses of alcohol is unjust and unreliable. When truly controlled doses can be administered—such as will be possible with tetrahydrocannabinol, then comparisons may have some validity. Then the legalization of marihuana might become a viable issue. Then, too, careful controls on its manufacture, distribution, taxation, permissible age for use and the like would have to be determined. And consider the problems when marihuana manufacturers (the tobacco industry?) and advertisers promote sales for their "new and improved" products!

The foreign reports that cannabism is a problem producing psychotic reactions requiring hospitalization in some users and lethargic, apathetic, ineffective, non-productive behavior in many others, have been noted. In Vietnam, the problem of psychotic reactions among U.S. soldiers using local marihuana is unclear. Are these cases the result of more potent marihuana resins (some are treated with opiates) or are the users psychologically prone to this reaction under war-stress? Will research with THC find what experienced observers and ex-users have noted? That is, among chronic (long-time) heavy users of marihuana (and other hallucinogens) these changes take place: problems in concentrating; failing memory; decrease in mathematics ability; increasing feelings of paranoia; significant increase or decrease in self-esteem; passivity or loss of energy; difficulty getting thoughts into words; impulsiveness; problems with personal relationships; feelings of futility; and a strong denial that drugs might be harmful. (11) Or, do these users display apathetic, unmotivated or anomic behavior before they become users? Does the drug experience support their "condition"?

At present, for somewhat obvious reasons, these drugs—hallucinogens—are illegal under the 1965 and 1968 Drug Abuse Control Amendments to the Federal Food, Drug and Cosmetic Act. Penalties for first offense of possession may be reduced from the earlier harsher restrictions. Nevertheless, hallucinogens in one form or another will be available in our society. The decision to use them or not is primarily an individual matter.

1. Can hallucinatory experiences be induced without drugs? How?
2. Do any of the hallucinogens produce physical dependence? How can they produce psychological dependence?
3. What are the "conditions" that affect the effects of drugs? Why should there be a "guide" for "trip-takers"?
4. Recall a frightening dream or nightmare. Did this cause physical symptoms? What were they? How is a dream or nightmare different from a drug-trip?
5. Survey the class or friends. How many instances of drug use can be identified with bad or harmful experiences?
6. Can you elaborate on the meaning of toxic psychosis?
7. In what (experimental) ways have hallucinogenic drugs been tried? What have been the results?

REFERENCES

1. LUDWIG, ARNOLD, M., M.D., and LEVINE, JEROME, M.D., "Patterns of Hallucinogenic Drug Abuse," *Journal of American Medical Association,* 191:104-108, January 11, 1965.
2. WOLF, HAROLD H., Ph.D., "Pharmacological Effects of Drugs Subject to Abuse," *Drug Abuse: A Report of the Butler University Drug Abuse Institute,* Indianapolis, Indiana: Butler University, 1968, p. 50-59.
3. BARRON, FRANK, JARVIK, MURRAY E., and BUNNELL, STERLING, "The Hallucinogenic Drugs," *Scientific American,* 210:29-37, April, 1964.
4. SMITH, DAVID E., M.D., "Use of LSD in the Haight-Ashbury," *California Medicine,* 110:472-476, June, 1969.
5. Council on Mental Health and Committee on Alcoholism and Drug Dependence, "Dependence on LSD and other Hallucinogenic Drugs," *Journal of the American Medical Association,* 202:47-50, October 2, 1967.
6. ZELLWEGER, HANS, M.D., and others, "Is LSD a Teratogen?" *Lancet,* 2:1066-1068, November 18, 1967.
7. News of the Week, "Exencephalia," *Medical World News,* 10:8, January 31, 1969.
8. "Marihuana: The Law vs. 12 Million People," *Life,* 67:27-34, October 31, 1969. See also: "The Marihuana Problem: Pot Is Going Middle Class—With Profound Effects," *Newsweek,* July 24, 1967.
9. MERRILL, FREDERICK T., *Marihuana,* Washington, D. C.: Opium Research Committee, Foreign Policy Association, Inc., 1938, 48 pp.
10. "Drugs: The Trouble With THC," *Time,* January 24, 1969.
11. COHEN, ALLEN Y., "The Mystery of Psychedelic Drugs," A lecture presented at the College of Pharmacy, The Ohio State University, November 5, 1969.
12. COHEN, SIDNEY, M.D., "Pot, Acid, and Speed," *Medical Science,* 19:30-35, February, 1968.

CHAPTER 6

Stimulants

Stimulants—particularly those of the amphetamine type—are known as "ups" by many abusers. They are also called "pep pills," "eye-openers," "co-pilots," and "truck drivers," "L. A. turn-arounds," and "coast-to-coast." During World War II, pilots on long-range bombing missions sometimes used medically prescribed amphetamines to maintain alertness. Long-haul truck drivers abused amphetamines to stay awake in order to complete runs more quickly. Fatal highway accidents occurred as a result and the abuse of "pep pills"—illegally obtained—began to receive national attention. Amphetamines are prescribed also for astronauts who must stay awake and be able to perform critical tasks at certain stages of their long flights—particularly during re-entry into the earth's atmosphere.

Other names for amphetamines are related to their appearance (tablets) or their trade names: "peaches," "hearts," "roses," "footballs," "greenies," "bennies" (Benzedrine), and "dexies" (Dexedrine). Amphetamine in liquid form, for injection, is known as "jugs," "bottles," and "bombido." More recently the name "speed" has been used, particularly for the more potent forms such as Methamphetamine (Methedrine) also known as "Meth" and "Crystal." By now you have probably heard the truism "speed kills."

Amphetamine was synthesized and first used, more than 30 years ago, as a vasopressor—to provide temporary relief from the symptoms of a cold by shrinking nasal membranes. Effective drugs with fewer side effects are now available for this purpose. The over-the-counter nasal inhalators no longer contain amphetamine. This drug is a central nervous system stimulant which produces effects similar to the stimulation of the subsystem known as the sympathetic nervous system. It mimics the effects of the release of adrenalin (epinephrine in particular) and thus is known as a "sympathomimetic." That is, it inhibits the action of the smooth muscles of the intestines; excites the action of the smooth muscles of blood vessels supplying the skin and mucous membranes; excites the heart to increase heart rate and force of contraction (increases blood pressure); increases the metabolic conversion of glycogen into sugar in liver and muscle (releasing energy); stimulates the respiratory rate; induces wakefulness; dilates the pupils, and reduces appetite. Similar reactions occur when one is provoked to anger and prepares to fight—or run away in fear.

The medical uses of amphetamines include: controlling the symptoms of narcolepsy (a condition of uncontrollable attacks of sleep usually of short duration); controlling or calming (paradoxically) certain hyperkinetic or hyperactive children (perhaps by increasing their attention span thus enabling them to stay at one activity longer); relieving or preventing fatigue in individuals with deteriorated psychomotor performance; treating mild depression (elevating mood); counter-acting depressant drugs such as barbiturates and alcohol (particularly as in suicidal poisoning and alcoholism); controlling appetite (as an anorexiant to reduce food intake and help control weight); inducing insomnia and counteracting fatigue in the performance of tasks of long duration (as in astronauts); and, enhancing the action of analgesic (pain-relieving) drugs. (1) Since amphetamine also has a contractile effect on the sphincter of the bladder, it may be used to treat enuresis (bedwetting) and incontinence.

General Patterns of Abuse

Perhaps the greatest number of abusers includes dieting housewives and their hard-driving executive husbands. We cannot know—statistics are unavailable. Long-distance truck drivers have been recognized. College students in substantial numbers have used amphetamines to stay awake to study for exams. Athletes have been known to use amphetamines in attempts to improve performance. (Athletic associations have outlawed "doping" both as physically dangerous and as unsportsmanlike behavior). Barbiturate and alcohol users sometimes take amphetamines to "get themselves going again." A small but significant number of young (and young adult) "spree" abusers take amphetamines for "kicks" or as an "experience." Sometimes amphetamines and barbiturates are taken in combination or sequence—"ups" and "downs"—for the effects. "Shooting speed"—intravenous injections of methamphetamine at regular and frequent intervals is a severe form of abuse. "Speed freaks"— as they are called by "non-speeders"—claim they experience intense orgiastic and euphoric feelings called a "flash" or "rush." Criminals have been known to take pep pills for "courage" and alertness.

Since amphetamines are illegal unless medically prescribed, abusers obtain them by going to several physicians or on the black market. Some of it is illicitly manufactured, some is smuggled into the country, and much of it is stolen.

General Effects of Abuse

The amphetamines, in controlled amounts, are capable of producing changes for which they are prescribed. In addition to the reactions cited earlier, the user experiences increased sensory perception. Subjectively, he feels more energetic and self-confident and even believes his thought processes are faster and more efficient. He may experience a general feeling of well-being even of euphoria or, conversely, dysphoria. In some users it engenders unpleasant feelings and increased psychological tensions.

Continued use of amphetamines leads to the development of tolerance and larger doses are needed for desired effects. Unfortunately the effects will vary in individuals and become exaggerated. Restlessness, tremors, talkativeness, irritability, hyperactivity, lack of appetite, and insomnia are milder symptoms of abuse. Amphetamine psychosis—a paranoid state with auditory and visual hallucinations—has been observed on a single 50 milligram dose. Amphetamine intoxication in some abusers can precipitate a schizophrenic episode. Chronic abusers and "spree" abusers are more likely to experience amphetamine toxicity. More severe symptoms may include coma, convulsions, possible heart failure, and death. Several cases have been reported in which "speed" caused the death of its abuser and where violence committed by a "speed freak" led to murder. (2) (3) (An additional risk of "shooting" or "main-lining meth" are infections and hepatitis from unsterile hypodermics or injection techniques).

Sometimes, reports indicate occurrence of loss of memory and diminished ability to concentrate. Marked weight loss, abscesses, nonhealing ulcers and facial puffiness, probably due to malnourishment occurs in chronic abusers. Though sometimes used as a sex stimulant, abuse frequently leads to impotence.

Fortunately, amphetamines do not seem to cause physical dependence involving a characteristic abstinence syndrome. However, psychological dependence is characteristic of abuse.

> With all dangerous drugs, the principal hazards of self-medication is that the abuser often is incapable of accurately evaluating his performance and is likely to overmedicate—a practice that, in neurotic or dependence-prone persons, often leads to chronic abuse. (1)

Cocaine

Though legally defined a narcotic under the law, cocaine is pharmacologically a stimulant. (Not to be confused with "cacao" the tree from which cocoa and chocolate are obtained). Cocaine abuse occurs primarily among hard core "addicts"—those dependent upon narcotics such as opium and its derivatives. The coca bush is found in the Andes mountains of South America where Peruvians, Bolivians, and Chileans are known to chew its leaves for its (mild) stimulating effect. When processed in illegal laboratories it is transformed to a more powerful form—a white, crystalline powder—and is smuggled into the states.

Known as "snow," it is also called "Coke," "Cholly," "Charlie," "happy dust," "gold dust," "Corine," "Bernice," and "flake," to name a few.

Once widely used as a local anesthetic in medicine and dentistry, it has been replaced by newer less toxic drugs. In sufficient doses—taken by sniffing the powder and sometimes by "mainlining"—it stimulates the brain and central nervous system. In addition to the usual physical symptoms the abuser is highly active, talkative and euphoric. Hallucinations are also experienced. Sometimes heroin is mixed with cocaine for its heightened effects. This is known as "speedball." Depression or "let down" suddenly follows stimulation. Overdosages can depress respiratory function causing death. Though physical dependence is not characteristic of cocaine abuse, there is a very strong psychological dependence. It is believed that psychologically disturbed or psychotic types prefer cocaine.

Discussion

Obviously amphetamine use and abuse is not uncommon. Johnny Cash, currently the foremost singer of country music, was hooked on amphetamines. (4) Before his meteoric rise to fame his habit was so strong "he woke up in a Georgia jail unable to remember how he got there." While Cash is fortunate, his story unfortunately serves the interests of those who believe "it only happens to others, it can't happen to me." Getting hooked on a drug habit is an insidious process like learning to smoke cigarettes. Using amphetamines for weight-control is effective, if at all, only in the early stages of a diet-activity program. Sustained success depends upon modifying eating patterns and food choices.

Amphetamines are not a source of energy but they can drive the user to prolonged expenditures of his own energies while disguising the beneficial signs of fatigue. Extended to exhaustion while driving a car or truck or while flying leads to fatal accidents. Athletes—bicycle racers—in France, using amphetamines suffered fatal heart attacks. Students "cramming" for exams all night on pep pills may increase their output but they are less accurate and their judgement is impaired. (5)

Though the effects of amphetamines vary among individuals, it is necessary to remember that under proper pharmacologic conditions, these drugs are beneficial to man. All we need to know is how to control "conditions." Do you know?

REFERENCES

1. Committee on Alcoholism and Addiction and Council on Mental Health, "Dependence on Amphetamines and Other Stimulant Drugs," *Journal of the American Medical Association*, 197:1023-1027, September 19, 1966.
2. "Speed Kills," *Time*, October 20, 1967, p. 23.

1. Under what circumstances would you consider the continued use of amphetamines?

2. Why do you suppose "hippies" who do not use "speed" call those who do "speed freaks"?

3. Have you used amphetamines for weight-control or other prescribed purposes? Describe their effects and your results.

4. Have you tried amphetamines as an aid to all night study sessions? Describe their effects and your results.

5. What are the similarities, if any, between amphetamines and hallucinogens?

3. ZALIS, EDWIN G., M.D., and PARMLEY, LOREN F. JR., M.D., "Fatal Amphetamine Poisoning," *Archives of Internal Medicine,* 112:822-826, December, 1963.
4. DEARMORE, TOM, "First Angry Man of Country Singers," *New York Times Magazine,* September 21, 1969, Section 6, p. 32-39, 42-49, 54-58. See also: "Hard-Times King of Songs," *Life,* 67:44-48 November 21, 1969.
5. "Amphetamine Test Blurs Judgement in Students," *Medical Tribune,* September 9, 1964.

CHAPTER 7

Depressants

A variety of unrelated drugs comprise this group—depressants—also known as sedatives and hypnotics. Sedatives act to produce a calming effect and hypnotics act to induce sleep. The difference, however, may be a matter of degree. Depending upon the dose, the same drug can have both effects.

Alcohol is a commonly known and widely used central nervous system (brain) depressant. Antihistamines used to control cold and allergy symptoms produce drowsiness as a side effect. Some are used to control motion sickness (we hope the car driver doesn't need large doses!) Bromides were in use over one hundred and fifty years ago as sedatives and are available over-the-counter as tension reducers and headache relievers. Severe habituation and intoxication leading to mental disturbance and even death are known to result from bromide abuse. Scopolamine, a mild sedative derived from belladonna, is sometimes combined with bromides, antihistamine (methapyrilene), and pain-killers such as salicylamide and acetophenatidin and sold as "tranquilizers" and sleeping pills. (1) Scopolamine has been used with medical narcotics before operations but in too high doses it is toxic and can cause euphoria, hallucinations, amnesia and delirium. Chloral hydrate ("knock-out drops" or "Mickey Finn") commercially known as Somnos was recognized as a sedative since 1869.

Tranquilizers are a newer group of sedatives developed synthetically in the last twenty years to reduce tension and anxiety without impairing mental or physical ability. The "major" tranquilizers such as the phenothiazines are used as antipsychotic agents. Thorazine and Compazine are examples of tranquilizers used to treat schizophrenics—not as a cure but to enable them to function better and make them amenable to psychiatric treatment. Since the use of these psychotropic agents in 1955, the patient population in mental hospitals has dramatically declined. The length of hospital stay has been reduced and more out-patient care was made possible. (2) Of course, not all mental illness is helped by tranquilizers.

The natural "tranquilizer" used for centuries was the snakeroot rauwolfia from which we have extracted reserpine, the active element. In India, snakeroot was used to treat many ailments. Today reserpine is used primarily to control high blood pressure.

The "minor" tranquilizers consist of different chemical compounds such as meprobamate, commercially known as Equanil and Miltown, chlordiazepoxide or Librium, and diazepam known as Valium. There are numerous others also used to reduce anxiety, control convulsions, relax muscles, reduce heart rate, and control mild behavior disorders. Also sleep may be induced by relief of tension. The "major" tranquilizers are apparently not widely abused. However, the "minor" tranquilizers, though they do not produce euphoria, are subject to abuse. They have an intoxicating effect especially in combination with alcohol. Driving a car while under their influence can be dangerous. In those psychologically predisposed a psychic dependence can develop. In addition, with some of these drugs, tolerance can develop and repeated large doses over time can cause physical dependence. Sudden withdrawal may result in convulsions and requires medical attention. Overdoses of meprobamate (10 to 20 times prescribed daily dose) can be lethal. Under proper medical supervision the tranquilizers can usually be used for long periods of time without undue effect.

Barbiturates

Most widely abused among the depressants (except for alcohol) are the barbiturates. More than two thousand derivatives of barbituric acid have been synthesized since its introduction over 100 years ago. The first barbiturate hypnotic was introduced in 1903 as barbital known commercially as Veronal. Phenobarbital, known commercially as Luminal, is another long-acting hypnotic. Short-to-intermediate-acting—in terms of duration of action—are secobarbital (or Seconal), pentobarbital (or Nembutal), and amobarbital (or Amytal). These came into use in the last 30 years and are most subject to abuse. Very short-acting thiopental (Pentothal) is used for anesthesia.

Medically, barbiturates are sedative-hypnotics used to produce sleep or treat insomnia, reduce mental tension or anxiety (and as an aid to psychotherapy), treat hyperthyroidism and high blood pressure, and to control epilepsy and the convulsions which may be caused by other toxic drugs.

General Patterns of Barbiturate Abuse

Individuals seeking "relief from tension" or a night's repose, may prevail upon their physician for "some sleeping pills." In the past, physicians may have contributed to their dependence on barbiturates. The current Drug Abuse Amendment Law helps to control this "misuse" of drugs which can lead to abuse. Other individuals, using stimulants for weight-control or other reasons, have felt a need for depressants so they could sleep and a vicious cycle of abuse is started. If they become habituated—psychologically dependent—they may visit several physicians or begin to obtain their "barbs" illegally.

On the street, abusers know barbiturates as "candy," "goofballs," "peanuts" or by their colors and trade names—"yellow jackets" or "nimbies," "reds," "Red Devils" or "seccy," "rainbows," and "blue birds." The combination or sequential abuse of "downs" was mentioned earlier with the "ups" or amphetamines.

Four main types of barbiturate abusers have been identified. (3) There are those who seek almost total oblivion and semipermanent stupor to escape emotional distress; those who seek the paradoxical excitation—feelings of exhilaration—produced after tolerance has developed or in some cases without tolerance; those who abuse barbiturates with amphetamines; and, those who abuse them with alcohol and other drugs—particularly narcotic abusers when opiates are not available.

General Effects of Barbiturate Abuse

At moderate doses, intoxication like that of alcohol may be experienced. Euphoria and disinhibition can occur. Some experience excitement rather than sedation and others may feel dizzy and nauseous. Notably, an individual may react differently to the drug at different times and perhaps moreso at different dosages.

Excessive dosages would be noted by slurring of speech, staggering, loss of balance, quick temper, and a quarrelsome disposition—sometimes seen in alcohol intoxication. Long term usage leads to the development of tolerance requiring increasing quantities to obtain the desired effects.

Normally, barbiturates only slightly depress respiration and decrease blood pressure and heart rate. In large doses, however, these functions may be significantly reduced and coma induced. Death due to unintentional or accidental "suicide" may result from toxic overdose especially when combined with other depressants such as alcohol. An estimated 3000 deaths occur this way each year and several famous persons have died, notably Alan Ladd, Dorothy Kilgallen, and Marilyn Monroe. No suicide notes were found. It is assumed that errors in perception of time (due to intoxication) and a slow absorption rate combined to cause the victims to accidentally and stuporously consume lethal doses while trying to obtain the desired effect. Normal sedative doses range from about 50 to 200 milligrams per day depending upon the barbiturate used and other conditions. Five to ten times the daily dose can be fatal.

Lethal doses aside, barbiturate abuse is associated with psychopathology, which is difficult to treat and subject to frequent relapse. (3) Physical dependency develops and is extremely dangerous. Doses of 800 mg. per day for several weeks can lead to severe physical dependence. This in turn is associated with additional psychopathology.

1. Have you ever purchased a depressant such as antihistamine or bromide? How can you determine what type of drugs are contained in your purchase?
2. If you have had some experience in the use of depressants—including alcohol—can you describe their effects?
3. What is characteristic of the names of barbiturates? How many drugs with barbiturate-like action can you identify?
4. Are you familiar with someone using medically prescribed depressants? For what purposes are they used?
5. How can the abuse of barbiturates be avoided? List some steps you would take.
6. Would barbiturate abusers be worse off than amphetamine abusers? If so, in what ways? If not, why not?

Withdrawal syndrome is apparent upon sudden withdrawal of barbiturates from the physically "addicted." Severity of withdrawal varies with the degree of dependence. Early effects are anxiety, headache, muscle twitching, weakness, impaired cardiovascular response when standing, and vomiting. After 24 hours they are more severe. In the second day, convulsion (like grand mal epilepsy seizures) occur. Increased insomnia, delirium, disorientation, and hallucinations occur at times. Though untreated, complete clinical recovery is possible. However, deaths have occurred during uncontrolled, untreated barbiturate withdrawal. This condition is considered more dangerous than withdrawal from opiate narcotics.

Discussion

Because of their wide use in medicine, sedative-hypnotics—particularly barbiturates—are believed by many to be harmless sleeping pills. Obviously, in controlled doses they are extremely beneficial. These psychoactive drugs have done a great deal to reduce mental illness, control behavior and neurological disorders, and alleviate some physical symptoms.

As with so many of man's discoveries, inventions, and innovations the benefits of drugs are accompanied by hazards—the advantages with disadvantages. A continuing task is learning to take advantage of the former while reducing the latter to its absolute minimum.

REFERENCES

1. BERLAND, THEODORE, "Quiet Pills Are No Short Cut!", *Today's Health*, 34:68-69, October, 1961.
2. AYD, FRANK J., JR., "Are Psychoactive Drugs Worthwhile?", *Medical Counterpoint*, 1:35-37, April, 1969.
3. Committee on Alcoholism and Addiction, "Dependence on Barbiturates and Other Sedative Drugs," *Journal of the American Medical Association*, 193:673-677, August 23, 1965.

CHAPTER 8

Narcotics

(Editor's note: For this chapter we are indebted to the Bureau of Narcotics and Dangerous Drugs of the U.S. Department of Justice for their permission. The following is adapted from their Fact Sheet 6.)

Narcotic Drugs

The term narcotic generally refers to opium and drugs made from opium, such as heroin, codeine and morphine. These drugs are distilled from the juice of the base of the poppy flower and refined into some of the most valuable medicines known to man, but also some of the most thoughtlessly abused drugs in the world. In addition other drugs have been included under the federal law as narcotics, which are pharmacologically entirely different from the opium derivatives. An example of this is cocaine, which is a derivative of the coca leaf and a stimulant to the central nervous system. Additionally, a number of specially defined synthetic drugs, called "opiates," are also classified as narcotic drugs under the federal law.

MEDICINAL NARCOTICS: Natural and synthetic morphine-like drugs are the most effective pain relievers known. They are among the most valuable drugs available to physicians and are widely used for short-term acute pain resulting from surgery, fractures, burns, etc., as well as to reduce suffering in the later stages of terminal illnesses such as cancer. In fact, morphine is used as the standard of pain relief by which other narcotic drugs are evaluated.

These drugs depress the central nervous system to produce a marked reduction in sensitivity to pain, drowsiness, sleep, and reduce physical activity. Side effects can include nausea and vomiting, constipation, itching, flushing, constriction of pupils and respiratory depression.

Manufacture and distribution of medicinal opiates are stringently controlled by the Federal government through laws designed to keep these products available only for legitimate medical use. Those who distribute these drugs are registered with Federal authorities and must comply with specific record-keeping and drug security requirements.

45

ABUSE: The abuse of narcotic drugs dates from ancient times and its seriousness has increased with the years. The appeal of morphine-like drugs lies in their ability to reduce sensitivity to both psychological and physical stimuli and to produce a sense of euphoria. They dull fear, tension and anxiety. Under the influence of morphine-like narcotics, the addict is usually lethargic and indifferent to his environment and personal situation.

Chronic use leads to both physical and psychological dependence. Tolerance develops and ever-increasing doses are required in order to achieve the desired effect. As the need for the drug increases, the addict's activities become increasingly drug-centered.

When the drug supplies are cut off, withdrawal symptoms may develop. Characteristically they may include nervousness, anxiety, sleeplessness, yawning, running eyes and nose, sweating; enlargement of the pupils, "gooseflesh," muscle twitching; severe aches in back and leg muscles, hot and cold flashes; vomiting, diarrhea, increase in breathing rate, blood pressure and temperature, and a feeling of desperation and an obsessional desire to secure a "fix." However, the intensity of withdrawal symptoms varies with the degree of physical dependence and the amount of drug customarily used. Typically the symptoms begin about 8 to 12 hours after the last dose. They increase in intensity and reach a peak in 36 to 72 hours. At this point the symptoms of withdrawal gradually diminish over the next 5 to 10 days, but insomnia, nervousness and muscle aches and pains may last for several weeks.

Addicts live under the perpetual threat of an overdose. This can happen in several ways. An addict may miscalculate the strength of his dose or the drug may be stronger than it was represented to be at the time the addict bought it. Death from narcotic overdosage is caused by respiratory depression.

Although the possibility of death from an overdose of narcotics is an ever-constant danger to the addict the harmful effects to the addict are usually indirect. Because addicts do not feel hungry, they often suffer from malnutrition. Because they are pre-occupied with drug-taking addicts usually neglect themselves. They are more apt to contract infections because their nutritional status is poor and because they may inject contaminated drugs intravenously and are likely to be using poor or unsterile injection techniques. This may result in serious or fatal septicemia (blood-poisoning), hepatitis, and abscesses of the liver, brain and lungs.

HEROIN: Known to the addict as "H," "boy," "horse," "white stuff," "Harry," "hairy," "joy powder," or "doojee," heroin produces an intense euphoria making it the most popularly abused narcotic. Similar to all narcotic drugs, a tolerance develops rapidly and the abuser must ingest increasingly larger quantities to get his "kicks."

Heroin is usually mixed into a liquid solution and injected into a vein, the process is called "mainlining." While other methods of administration are by mouth or by inhalation, "mainlining" gives the most pronounced and rapid effect. The first emotional reaction is an easing of fears and relief from worry. This is often followed by a state of inactivity bordering on stupor.

Heroin is synthesized from morphine, and grain for grain, is up to ten times more potent in its pharmacologic effects. Pure heroin is "cut" or diluted by the trafficker with substances like milk sugar or quinine or both. By the time the drug is sold to the addict the heroin content ranges from 3 to 10%.

MORPHINE: Morphine is called "white stuff," "M," "hard stuff," "morpho," "unkie," and "Miss Emma" by the street addict. It is the drug of choice for relief of pain, but takes second place to heroin as a drug of abuse. Still, morphine is widely used by addicts, particularly when heroin is difficult to obtain. Euphoria can be produced with small doses and tolerance builds rapidly.

CODEINE: More commonly abused in the form of the exempt narcotic cough preparations, codeine is less addictive than morphine or heroin and less potent in terms of inducing euphoria. When withdrawal symptoms occur, they are less severe than with the more potent drugs.

HYDROCODONE (Dihydrocodeinone): When classed as an exempt preparation, hydrocodone was fairly popular. However, since its classification as a narcotic, little effort has been expended in obtaining the drug in any great quantity.

HYDROMORPHONE (Dihydromorphinone): Hydromorphone, like morphine, is the next choice after heroin. Although almost as potent as heroin, the drug does not appear to have the thrill associated with mainlining heroin.

MEPERIDINE: When first produced this drug was claimed to be without addicting potential. Experience, however, proved otherwise (as it did with morphine and heroin). Addiction is slower to develop and less intense than with morphine.

OXYCODONE (Dihydrohydroxcodeinone): Oxycodone has recently been classisfied as a drug with high addiction potential. Although effective orally, most addicts dissolve tablets in water, filter out the insoluble binders and "mainline" the active drug.

EXEMPT NARCOTICS: Under Federal law, some preparations containing small amounts of narcotic drugs may be sold without a prescription. The reason for their exemption lies in the fact that very large quantities of such preparations would have to be consumed regularly over a considerable time to produce significant dependence. Pharmacists selling exempt preparations must have a Federal narcotic stamp.

The best known of these exempt narcotics are paregoric and certain cough mixtures. Paregoric is a liquid preparation which contains an opium extract and is used primarily to counteract diarrhea. Exempt cough mixtures containing codeine are useful in suppressing irritation or uncontrollable cough in certain upper respiratory infections.

1. What "life-style" would you associate with the inhabitants or frequenters of the Chinese opium dens of the past?

2. If you were to exercise a choice of drug dependence would you choose heroin? Why or why not?

3. Which drug would you choose to abuse? Why?

4. Why would you not choose any drug to abuse?

5. Are you familiar with drug rehabilitation organizations such as Synanon and Encounter? What are they? How do they operate?

Although these preparations are reasonably safe and free of addiction potential when used as directed, they can be abused. Addicts will sometimes turn to paregoric or cough syrups—as well as other drugs—when heroin is in short supply, but large quantities must be consumed by addicts when substituted for the more potent drugs.

Discussion

The foregoing by the Bureau of Narcotics and Dangerous Drugs and "common knowledge" provides most people—even abusers of other drugs—with an aversion to narcotic "addiction." Nevertheless, the narcotic problem, though smaller in quantity than other drug problems is highly significant and of considerable consequence. More recent estimates indicate there may be as many as 100,000 dependent on narcotics in New York City alone. A famous professional football player in Baltimore died of an overdose. But in New York City, in 1968, 650 in the age group 15 to 35 years died of causes associated with heroin abuse.[1] A greater number of deaths is anticipated for 1969. The death of a 12 year old boy—due to an overdose of heroin (perhaps a stronger dose from a new source)—has been reported. Hepatitis may be reaching epidemic proportions among men and women "mainliners."

REFERENCES

1. "Heroin and Death," *Time*, July 11, 1969, p. 38.

CHAPTER 9

Drugs and the Law

(Editor's note: For this chapter we are indebted to the Bureau of Narcotics and Dangerous Drugs of the U.S. Department of Justice for their permission. The following is adapted from their Fact Sheet 2 and Fact Sheet 11.)

Federal Narcotic and Marihuana Laws, Controlled Drugs

The term "narcotic drugs," includes opium and its derivatives such as heroin and morphine; coca leaves and its derivatives, principally cocaine; and the "opiates" which are specially defined synthetic narcotic drugs. Four principal statutes—the Narcotic Drugs Import and Export Act, the Harrison Narcotic Act, the Narcotics Manufacturing Act of 1960 and the Marihuana Tax Act—control narcotic drugs and marihuana. These laws are designed to insure an adequate supply of narcotics for medical and scientific needs, while at the same time they are planned to curb, if not prevent, the abuse of narcotic drugs and marihuana. In addition to these laws, there are other Federal legislative measures to lend additional control over narcotic drugs. Since, however, they are designed primarily to aid enforcement of the major statutes, they are not discussed here.

NARCOTIC DRUGS IMPORT AND EXPORT ACT: The Narcotic Drugs Import and Export Act authorizes the import of crude opium and coca leaves for medical and scientific needs in the United States. Import of other narcotic drugs is prohibited. Manufactured drugs and preparations may be exported under a rigid system of controls to assure that the drugs are used for medical needs only in the country of destination.

HARRISON NARCOTIC ACT: The Harrison Narcotic Act sets up the machinery for distribution of narcotic drugs within the country. Under the law, all persons who import, manufacture, produce, compound, sell, deal in, dispense or transfer narcotic drugs must be registered and pay a graduated occupational tax. The law also imposes a commodity tax upon narcotic drugs produced in or imported into the United States and sold or removed for consumption or sale.

Under the Harrison Act, sales or transfers of narcotic drugs must be recorded on an official order form. However, the transfer of narcotic drugs from a qualified practitioner to his patient and the sale of these drugs from a pharmacist to a patient with a lawfully written doctor's prescription are exceptions to this requirement.

NARCOTICS MANUFACTURING ACT OF 1960: The Narcotics Manufacturing Act of 1960 develops a system of licensing manufacturers to produce narcotic drugs. It also provides a method to set manufacturing quotas for the basic classes of narcotic drugs, both natural and synthetic, insuring that an adequate supply of each drug will be available for medicine and science.

MARIHUANA TAX ACT: The Marihuana Tax Act requires all persons who import, manufacture, produce, compound, sell, deal in, dispense, prescribe, administer, or give away marihuana to register and pay a graduated occupational tax. No commodity tax is imposed on this drug. However, a tax is imposed upon all transfers of marihuana at the rate of $1 per ounce, or fraction of an ounce, if the transfer is made to a taxpayer registered under the act.

PENALTY PROVISIONS: Illegal sale or illegal importation of all narcotic drugs and marihuana can mean a penalty of 5 to 20 years in prison and the possibility of a $20,000 fine in addition. A second or subsequent offense receives a penalty of 10 to 40 years in prison with a possible $20,000 fine. There can be no probation or suspension of these offenses.

The penalty for all so-called possession type of offenses range between 2 and 10 years in prison for the first offense and between 5 and 20 years for the second offense. For a third or subsequent offense, the penalty can be from 10 to 40 years in prison. There can be no probation or suspension of sentence for a second or subsequent offense.

Because of the serious nature of narcotic addiction among young persons, the law establishes special penalties for the sale of narcotic drugs to a minor. The penalty for unlawful sale of heroin to a minor by an adult is a 10 year mandatory sentence in prison, while a penalty of 10 to 40 years in prison is levied when marihuana or other narcotic drugs are sold to a minor.

In 1966 special legislation was enacted to allow those violators who are narcotic addicts to return to useful, productive lives. The Narcotic Rehabilitation Act provides: (1) civil commitment of certain addicts in lieu of prosecution for Federal offenses, (2) sentencing of addicts to commitment for treatment after conviction of Federal offenses, (3) civil commitment of persons not charged with any criminal offense, (4) rehabilitation and posthospitalization care programs and assistance to States and localities and (5) availability of parole to all marihuana violators presently incarcerated or subsequently convicted under Federal law.

All states have either adopted the Uniform Narcotic Act recommended in 1937 for the specific purpose of making all state narcotic laws analogous, or modified it to fulfill the state's individual needs.

Similar to the Federal laws, state laws restrict legitimate traffic to qualified manufacturers, wholesalers, druggists, practitioners and researchers.

FEDERAL DANGEROUS DRUG LAWS: Three groups of dangerous drugs—depressants, stimulants, and hallucinogens—are controlled by the Drug Abuse Control Amendments to the Federal Food, Drug and Cosmetic Act passed in 1965 and amended in 1968.

DRUG ABUSE CONTROL AMENDMENTS: These amendments control drug abuse in two ways. One, they provide for stronger regulations in the manufacture, distribution, delivery, and possession. Two, they provide strong criminal penalties against persons who deal in these drugs illegally.

Thus, all registered manufacturers, processors and their suppliers, wholesaler druggists, pharmacies, hospitals, clinics, public health agencies, and research laboratories must take an inventory, keep accurate records of receipts and sales of these drugs and make their records available to Bureau of Narcotics and Dangerous Drug agents for examination. No prescription for a controlled drug older than six months can be filled nor can refills be made more than five times in the six month period.

PENALTY PROVISIONS: Illegal possession of the dangerous drugs can mean a maximum penalty of one year in prison or a $1,000 fine, or both. However, the offender may be placed on probation for a first offense. If he meets the condition of his probation, the court may set aside his conviction. A second offense allows for probation, but does not allow for the conviction to be set aside. The third offense calls for a maximum prison term of three years or a fine of $10,000 or both.

A person who illegally produces, counterfeits, sells, manufactures or possesses dangerous drugs with intent to sell, may receive a maximum penalty of not more than five years in prison or a $10,000 fine or both.

Because of the serious consequences of drug abuse among young people, special penalties are provided for those over 18 years of age who sell or give any of the controlled drugs to persons under the age of 21. The first offense carries a maximum penalty of 10 years in prison, or a fine of $15,000, or both; a second offense increases the maximum prison term to 15 years, or a fine of not more than $20,000, or both.

Many states have adopted legislation for dangerous drugs similar to the controls at the Federal level.

The drugs subject to the provisions of the Drug Abuse Control Amendments to the Federal Food, Drug, and Cosmetic Act are known as depressant, stimulant, and hallucinogenic drugs.

"Depressant or stimulant drug" is defined under the Federal Food, Drug, and Cosmetic Act as:

"1. any drug which contains any quantity of
    a. barbituric acid or any of the salts of barbituric acid; or
    b. any derivative of barbituric acid which has been designated as habit forming;

2. any drug which contains any quantity of
   a. amphetamine or any of its optical isomers;
   b. any salt of amphetamine or any salt of an optical isomer of amphetamine; or
   c. any substance which by regulation has been designated as habit forming because of its stimulant effect on the central nervous system; or
3. lysergic acid diethylamide and any other drug which contains any quantity of a substance which by regulation has been designated as having a potential for abuse because of its depressant or stimulant effect on the central nervous system or its hallucinogenic effect. . . ."

The barbiturates and amphetamines listed in items (1) and (2) were controlled on February 1, 1966.

Additional drugs have been controlled under the Amendments because they have a potential for abuse because of their depressant, stimulant, or hallucinogenic effect. The drugs and dates of control:

Depressants

Chloral betaine (Beta-Chlor) 11/19/66
Chloral hydrate (Chloral) 05/18/66
Chlorhexadol (Lora) 11/19/66
Ethchlorvynol Placidyl) 05/18/66
Ethinamate (Valmid) 05/18/66
Glutethimide (Doriden) 05/18/66
Lysergic acid 09/11/66
Lysergic acid amide 09/11/66
Methyprylon (Noludar) 05/18/66
Paraldehyde 05/18/66
Petrichloral (Periclor) 11/19/66
Sulfondiethylmethane (Tetronal) 11/19/66
Sulfonethylmethane (Trional) 11/19/66
Sulfonmethane (Sulfonal) 11/19/66

Stimulants

d-, dl-Methamphetamine (d-, dl-Desoxyephedrine)
   and their salts 05/18/66
Phenmetrazine and its salts (Preludin) 09/21/66

Hallucinogens (Available only to qualified clinical investigators)

DMT (Dimethyltryptamine) 05/18/66
LSD; LSD-25 (d-Lysergic acid diethylamide) 05/18/66

1. What are the penalties for use, possession, or sale of illegal drugs in your state?
2. Do you know the differences between a misdemeanor and a felony? What are they? How do they affect individuals?
3. What is the most recent status of the Federal drug abuse law? When was it enacted?
4. What kinds of drug use are encouraged; tolerated; and punished?

Mescaline and its salts 05/18/66
Peyote (Provisions of the law do not apply to non-drug
    use in bona fide religious ceremonies of the
    Native American Church) 05/18/66
Psilocybin; psilocibin 05/18/66
Psilocyn; psilocin 05/18/66
DET (N-Diethyltryptamine) and its salts 11/22/67
Bufotenine and its salts 11/22/67
Ibogaine and its salts 11/22/67
DOM ("STP") 4-methyl-2, 5-dimethoxyamphetamine 04/02/68
THC—Tetrahydrocannabinols
    ("synthetic marihuana") 09/21/68

Discussion

The law is society's means of controlling deviant behavior which is considered dangerous to itself and its individuals. Sometimes society overreacts to behavioral phenomena and passes highly restrictive laws. Sometimes it underreacts and fails to enforce the existing laws. In different communities there are different laws and their application differs.

Religion, customs, manners, and social standards provide other kinds of "laws" or "rules" for acceptable behavior. The composite of these requirements and guides for behavior establish a sense of morality and define deviance. These are the "norms" or "mores" of society. Drug abusers are subject to these conventions.

Admonitions not to "meth" around are often futile in the face of the complex motivations for drug abuse. Whether drugs "turn you on" or "turn on you" may remain to be seen. At the very least, as "Mezz" Mezzrow, the once famous jazz musician of an earlier era had said, "I know at least one bad thing tea can do—it can put you in jail."

CHAPTER 10

Physiologic Considerations of the Nervous System

By Allan M. Burkman, Ph.D.

(Editor's note: For permission to reproduce this chapter, we are indebted to Dr. Burkman of The Ohio State University and to Melvin H. Weinswig, Ph.D., Editor of the Report of the Butler University Drug Abuse Institute, June 1968, in which this work appears.)

I. Introduction

All living matter is, in a unique way, excitable and responsive to changes that go on inside and outside of it. At birth and throughout life an individual is the recipient of continuous stimulation from the environment which forms and structures "reality" for him. Indeed, sustained contact with environmental stresses seems to be essential for the development of man's capacity to perceive stimuli and to respond appropriately.

The individual maintains contact with the environmental milieu by means of a nervous system, a complex organization of specialized cells that also serves to integrate and modulate activities of most of the other systems of the body. Furthermore, we must acknowledge as having special relevance to this symposium the fact that the highly irritable nervous system is a susceptible target for a variety of drugs which can be regarded as environmentally-derived chemical stimuli. These chemicals can often intensify, depress or distort nervous function. *How* chemical stimuli provoke nerve cell responses is not always clear. Certainly there are glaring deficiencies in our understanding of how drugs act. Yet considerable information is available concerning the site or locus of drug action, the way nerve cells behave in the presence of drugs and the manner in which normal nerve function is altered or disturbed. In order to take profitable advantage of the information that is available and to get some insight into the physiological consequences of drug use it is necessary to consider some of the characteristics of the nervous system that give it uniqueness and that make it susceptible to drug imposition.

II. The Nerve Cell

To keep the various parts of anything as complicated as the human organism operating properly requires a correspondingly complex co-ordinating device and the nervous system undoubtedly qualifies as the most complex of all body systems. Although their interrelationships may be exceedingly complex, the excitable nerve cells, or neurons, that constitute the working elements of the nervous system are all fundamentally similar. They are similar in the sense that they (1) have a common embryological origin (ectoderm), (2) consist of a relatively large nucleated cell mass or cell body from which emerge thread-like extensions called fibers which may be several feet in length, (3) are exquisitely sensitive to a variety of stimuli, and (4) possess the ability to conduct excitatory currents of energy from one end of the cell to another with very high velocity (up to 300 feet per second). The nervous system contains billions of nerve cells arranged in a complicated network that permits the uninterrupted propagation of excitatory waves from nerve cell to nerve cell so that an excitatory current generated by a stimulus at one part of the body may be transmitted to a distant part. The nerve cell fibers are often classified both on a structural and functional basis into two groups: (1) the dendrites consisting of one or more processes, usually branched, that convey the excitatory impulses *toward* the cell body and (2) a single axon, usually very long, that conducts impulses *away* from the cell body. The term "nerve," as it is conventionally used, refers to a bundle of axons, dendrites or both bound together by connective tissue sheaths.

III. Conduction and Transmission

A stimulus, defined as any disturbing influence to which a neuron is sensitive, triggers a series or chain of electro-chemical reactions that is propagated over the surface membrane of the nerve cell. This wave of reactivity is the nerve *impulse* and its propagation along the neuronal fiber is called *conduction*. Although a nerve cell can be stimulated anywhere along its length, stimulation normally occurs at one end only and from here impulses pass along the fiber to the other end. Under normal conditions, then, the neuron as a whole conducts impulses in one direction.

The fibers of consecutive neurons in a chain do not come into physical contact with each other but rather are separated by a minute but distinct gap or space. This junctional gap or *synapse* represents an anatomic discontinuity that would prevent uninterrupted impulse conduction from one nerve cell to the next were it not for the operation of an intricate synaptic mechanism. This mechanism effects the transfer of excitation between neurons and thus maintains the functional continuity of the impulse conduction phenomenon. The transfer of excitation across a synapse is described as *transmission*. A nerve impulse is transmitted from the tip of the axon of one neuron to the dendrite of the next across the synaptic junction by means of a chemical elaborated from the axon terminal. The chemical transmitter diffuses across the junctional gap and reacts with the dendritic membrane thereby initiating a new wave of excitation that is propagated over that neuron. The chemical transmitter is then degraded or diffuses away from the reactive sites and the original resting state is re-established. The arrival of another wave of excitation at the axon terminal of the first nerve cell will again trigger the release of small amounts of chemical that subserve the transmission event and will initiate an impulse in the second neuron.

Although there is still some debate about the nature of several potential transmitters, there is little doubt that two comparatively simple molecules, *acetylcholine* and *norepinephrine* (noradrenaline), that are synthesized and stored in nerve cells serve as chemical transmitters. There is also evidence that a third naturally-occurring substance, *5-hydroxytryptamine* (serotonin), may have transmitter capabilities. Biochemical distinctions can be made among nerve cells depending on the type of substance that is used as the transmitter. Nerve cells can be classed as cholinergic, adrenergic and possibly serotonergic. Neurons that utilize transmitter materials other than the three described would, of course, be classified independently.

IV. Organization and Integration

a. Receptors and Effectors

Receptors are cells or parts of cells that are especially sensitive to environmental stimuli. They are often highly selective in that only a specific kind and intensity of stimulus will influence and activate them. Sensations described as pressure, pain, temperature, taste, odor, vision and hearing represent distinct sensory experiences that result from the activation of specialized receptors. Receptors are the gateways to the nervous system and are associated with the dendritic terminals of many neurons. In some cases the dendrite terminals themselves are the receptors. Activation of these receptors will initiate the excitatory impulses that are conducted through the nerve cell. The neuron that has a receptor associated with it is called a *sensory neuron*. As a final consequence of nerve cell activity two general kinds of responses may be evoked. Muscles may react (contract or relax) and gland secretion may be altered (increased or decreased). These two types of structures are the only non-nervous elements that are innervated by and influenced by nervous activity and are described as *effectors*. The nerve cell that innervates and is associated with an effector is called a *motor neuron*. The synaptic mechanism for transmitting impulses from motor neuron to effector is, in all essential aspects, similar to that already described for interneuronal transmission.

Nerve cells that are not directly associated with either receptors or effectors but synapse only with other nerve cells are called *interneurons* or *connecting neurons.*

b. The Reflex Arc

A reflex can be described as an effector response to receptor stimulation mediated by sensory and motor neurons and, in many cases, multiple interneurons. Human behavior is largely an expression of reflex activities, some voluntary, some involuntary, some modified by conditioning and learning. The simplest kind of reflex event involves only a small number of nerve cells. The knee-jerk is a familiar example of a comparatively simple involuntary reflex. A slight blow (pressure) on the knee cap (actually the patellar ligament) when the legs are crossed will normally cause the foot to jerk forward. The response will not occur if the sensory neurons are damaged (as in locomotor ataxia or tabes dorsalis) or if motor nerve cell bodies and fibers are extensively damaged as in poliomyelitis.

The reflex response involves five structural elements that together make up the reflex arc—the functional unit of the nervous system. These include: (1) a sensory receptor, (2) a sensory neuron, (3) one or more connecting neurons, (4) a motor neuron and (5) an effector. The usual conception of a reflex arc includes a single sensory neuron transmitting impulses to a single motor cell via a connecting neuron. Actually, the simplest stimulus starts impulses through several sensory fibers with a volley of them following one another in rapid succession along each fiber. Each sensory fiber usually synapses with several connecting neurons which, in turn, synapse with several motor neurons. It is only when impulses arrive via several pathways at a motor neuron that the motor cell is finally activated. A certain intensity of stimulation must be produced at the synapse before the motor nerve cell reacts and conducts an impulse. In a sense, the synapses in a reflex arc serve as a barrier to the propagation of "trivial" impulses.

c. Central and Peripheral Systems

The billions of neurons that make up the nervous system are organized into anatomically defined categories: those belonging to the *central* nervous system (CNS) which includes the brain and spinal cord, and those belonging to the *peripheral nervous system* which includes all nervous elements outside the CNS (sensory receptors, nerve cell bodies of sensory and some motor neurons, dendrite and axon fibers). The CNS contains axons of sensory neurons, dendrites and nerve cell bodies of some motor neurons and most of the connecting nerve cells.

d. Development of Complexity

The nervous system begins as a very simple structure and is gradually modified in form and organization as it grows. It is often easier to appreciate the structural and functional relationships of the adult, i.e., fully developed, nervous system by considering what it was like at an early and simple stage and examining some of the changes that have taken place during growth and development that contribute to the increase in complexity.

In one of its most primitive embryonic stages the nervous system takes the form of a hollow blind tube. Groups of cells bud off from the main tubular structure, migrate varying distances and develop into neurons of the periphery. Fibers of some of these cells grow back into the tubular mass and so a connection is maintained between the peripheral elements and the tube. The hollow tube develops into the CNS. Fibers may grow out of the tube and either come to associate themselves synaptically with peripheral neurons or innervate effectors. Although differential changes in the size and shape of various parts of the primitive tube alter its appearance, even when fully developed the basis [sic] tubular geometry of the CNS remains evident.

The brain begins as a bulbous front end of the tube whose walls are composed of developing nerve cells. During development the smooth bulb is transformed into three distinct vesticles [sic] described as forebrain, midbrain, and hindbrain (technically called the prosencephalon, mesencephalon and rhombencephalon). The forebrain and hindbrain each form an additional bulb so that a five vesicle brain ultimately appears. Selective growth of certain regions accompanied by folding and flexing of the tube results in an adult brain that looks considerably different than it did during its earliest stages. A list of the five vesicles of the brain and their associated functions are presented in Tables 1 and 2. The tail end of the tube which undergoes virtually no regional alteration develops into the spinal cord retaining, even in its adult form, an obvious tubular pattern.

TABLE 1. *Principal Regions of the Adult Central Nervous System*

Forebrain (Prosencephalon)	Endbrain (Telencephalon)	Olfactory lobes Cerebral hemispheres
	Between brain (Diencephalon)	Thalamus Hypothalamus Pituitary stalk
Midbrain (Mesencephalon)		Acoustic & optic lobes
Hindbrain (Rhombencephalon)	After brain (Methencephalon)	Cerebellum Pons
	Cord brain (Myelencephalon)	Medulla oblongata
Spinal Cord		

TABLE 2. *Regions Associated with Specific Functions*

Olfactory lobes: Primitive "nose brain"; emotionally.

Cerebrum: Consciousness, insight, interpretation, recognition, memory, "personality."

Thalamus and Hypothalamus: Relay for ascending sensory impulses to cerebrum, regulation of body temperature, appetite, water balance, sleep, CHO and fat metabolism, external manifestations of emotion.

Midbrain acoustic/optic lobes: Centers for visual and auditory reflexes, regulates muscle tonus and posture, tracts to thalamus and cerebrum.

Cerebellum: Regulates muscle coordination, balance.

Pons: Bridge of crossed fibers coordinating activities of the cerebellum.

Medulla oblongata: Vegetative centers (respiratory, cardiac, vasomotor, vomiting, cough), tracts between cord and higher regions.

Spinal Cord: Ascending and descending tracts.

The working parts of the CNS are composed of neurons associated in groups for general and specialized functions. Thus, parts of the brain are occupied by neurons that control effectors in definite parts of the body and these neurons subserve definite functions. Although the CNS is bilaterally organized, there are numerous intercrossing fibers that insure synchronous actions of effectors on both sides of the body.

V. Sites at Which Drugs May Act

Drugs may produce distinct and sometimes selective effects because of their ability to reach specific regions of the nervous system with facility. Therefore, we attribute, in part, a drug's selectivity of effect to its ability to gain access preferentially to certain groups of neurons. The physico-chemical character of the drug molecule and the location of the neurons will determine accessibility. Of equal importance, of course, is the inherent physico-chemical character of the drug that confers upon it the intrinsic ability to influence a neuron in a highly selective way once contact becomes possible. Although drugs can act on different parts of a neuron it seems likely, based upon available evidence, that the synaptic sites represent the most important loci for drug action. Prevailing opinion (supported by substantial data) holds that many and perhaps most drugs exert their influence on the nervous system by influencing synaptic transmission. Drugs may influence transmission by (1) mimicing a normal chemical transmitter and exaggerating its effects, (2) preventing or enhancing synthesis, storage or release of a normal chemical transmitter, (3) accelerating the rate with which a transmitter is destroyed, (4) diminishing transmitter destruction, (5) preventing a liberated transmitter from reaching its reaction sites. There are many well documented examples of drugs which operate by one or more of these modes. A drug's ability to influence only cholinergic neurons will provoke responses that are quite different from those elicited by a drug that only effects adrenergic neurons. Similarly, a "cholinergic" drug that has access only to *some* cholinergic

1. Any questions?

neurons will produce effects that may be different from another "cholinergic" drug that does not have ready access to the same neurons. Selectivity based upon intrinsic activity and accessibility allows drugs to influence some body functions while sparing others. (1)

REFERENCES

1. BURKMAN, ALLAN M., "Physiological Considerations of the Nervous System," in *Drug Abuse: A Course for Educators,* A report of the Butler University Drug Abuse Institute, edited by Melvin H. Weinswig and Dale W. Doerr, Butler University, College of Pharmacy, Indianapolis, Indiana, 1968.

CHAPTER 11

Conclusion

This attempt to present "the facts" and provide some perspectives of drug abuse is all too brief. The issues of whether or not drug abuse is an illness or a crime; can drug abusers be rehabilitated; how effective are programs like Synanon and Encounter; what is the methadone treatment and why is it controversial, are some additional matters for your continuing interest and study. A Bibliography follows this chapter as an aid to broader perspectives.

Admittedly, objectivity on the subject of drug abuse is not only hard to find, it is a difficult posture to maintain. Like the reporting of news, we hear and are affected by mostly the bad and very little by the good. In any case, those emotionally committed to reject communication from the "establishment" will ignore such knowledge as there is and proceed to "do their thing." Whether out of self-respect or a respect for the "physical self" (body and mind), most individuals are reluctant to expose themselves and others to the risks and hazards of loss of self-control.

Many individuals can extrapolate from experiences with medicines, alcohol, and tobacco to an understanding or feeling of the drugged condition. Many can, by force of intellect, through reading, sympathize with the drug user but reject his life-style. Feelings and attitudes are often reinforced by portrayals of the drug dependent and the drug problem on television and in the motion pictures. Unfortunately, some of us insist on learning about drugs by direct experience.

An anti-drug message may have a greater impact from an ex-drug user or "addict." For what it is worth, many "acid-rock" musicians whose songs once espoused the use of drugs have now renounced them. The Beatles, Donovan, and Sonny Bono (of Sonny and Cher) have publicly announced their disenchantment and rejection of the drug scene. Many of this group are learning to turn on through the study of religion and mysticism or through a deeper involvement with others. For them, "Lucy In The Sky With Diamonds" has lost its lustre.

The rational individual—considered an unlikely candidate for drug abuse anyway—would wish to make decisions, chose behaviors, based on the most favorable probabilities. The information currently available enables the development of several concepts or generalizations which may serve as guidelines:

- —the effects of drugs, when abused, are unpredictable
- —a drug will affect different individuals in different ways
- —the same drug in the same amount may have a different effect on the same individual at different times
- —medically prescribed drugs, in therapeutic doses, are not likely to be harmful
- —"friends" rather than professional "pushers" are more likely to introduce you to drugs
- —there are advantages and disadvantages to the use of drugs, experiencing the former and minimizing the latter is a continuing problem.

Now its your turn. Use your brainpower to "conceptualize." Think up some concepts related to the characteristics of drug abusers, or the types of drugs, or of the social conditions associated with drug use. Read and discuss more of the "facts." Don't become a part of the problem, become involved in solving the problem. You won't need drugs to turn you on.

CHAPTER 12

A Brief Book Bibliography
to Expand the Mind

(For articles see References for each chapter)

General

BARBER, BERNARD, *Drugs and Society*. New York: Russell Sage Foundation, 1967.

BLUM, RICHARD H., and associates, *Society and Drugs*. Volume I, San Francisco: Jossey-Bass, Inc., Publishers, 1969.

————, *Students and Drugs*, Volume II, San Francisco: Jossey-Bass, Inc., Publishers, 1969.

DINITZ, SIMON, DYNES, R. R. and CLARK, A. C., *Deviance*. New York: Oxford University Press, 1969.

FARBER, S. M., and WILSON R., Editors, *Conflict and Creativity: Control of the Mind (Part II)*. New York: McGraw-Hill Paperbacks, 1963.

GOODMAN, L., and GILMAN, A. *The Pharmacological Basis of Therapeutics, 3rd Edition*. New York: Macmillan Company, 1965 (4th Edition in press).

LAURIE, PETER, *Drugs*. Baltimore: Penguin Books, 1967.

LOURIA, DONALD B., *Nightmare Drugs*. New York: Pocket Books, 1966.

NOWLIS, HELEN H., *Drugs on the College Campus*. New York: Anchor Books, 1969.

PROGER, SAMUEL, M.D., *The Medicated Society*. New York: The Macmillan Company, 1968.

WEINSWIG, MELVIN H., and DOERR, DALE W., editors, *Drug Abuse: A Course for Educators*. Indianapolis: Butler University, 1968.

Hallucinogens (LSD)

ALPERT, R., COHEN S., and SCHILLER L., *LSD*. New York: New American Library, 1966.

BLUM, RICHARD H., and associates, *Utopiates: The Use and Users of LSD-25*. New York: Atherton Press, 1964.

BRADEN, WILLIAM, *The Private Sea: LSD and the Search for God*. Chicago: Quadrangle Books, 1967.

COHEN, SIDNEY, *The Beyond Within: The LSD Story*. New York: Atheneum, 1964.

HOFFER, ABRAM, and OSMOND H., *The Hallucinogens*. New York: Academic Press, 1967.

LOURIA, DONALD B., *The Drug Scene*. New York: McGraw-Hill, 1968.

SOLOMON, DAVID, Editor, *LSD: The Consciousness-Expanding Drug*. New York: Putnam, Berkeley Medallion Books, 1964.

Young, Warren, and Hixson, J. R., *LSD on Campus*. New York: Dell, 1966.

Hallucinogens (Marihuana)

Bloomquist, Edward R., *Marihuana*. Beverly Hills: Glencoe Press, 1968.

Simmons, J. L., Editor, *Marihuana: Myths and Realities*. North Hollywood: Brandon House, 1967.

Solomon, David, Editor, *The Marihuana Papers*. Indianapolis: Bobbs-Merrill, 1966.

Wolstenholme, G. E. W., and Knight, J. Editors, *Hashish: Its Chemistry and Pharmacology*. Ciba Foundation Study, Boston: Little Brown, 1965.

Stimulants and Depressants

Kalant, O. J., *The Amphetamines: Toxicity and Addiction*. Springfield, Illinois: Charles C Thomas, Publisher, 1966.

Leake, Chauncey D., *The Amphetamines: Their Action and Uses*. Springfield, Illinois: Charles C Thomas, Publisher, 1958.

(See also items listed under General and Hallucinogens)

Narcotics

Chein, Isador, et al., *The Road to H.*, New York: Basic Books, 1964.

Kolb, Lawrence, *Drug Addiction*. Springfield, Illinois: Charles C Thomas, Publisher, 1962.

Lindesmith, Alfred A., *The Addict and The Law*. Bloomington: Indiana University Press, 1965.

————, *Addiction and Opiates*. Chicago: Aldine, 1968.

Maurer, David W., and Vogel, Victor H., *Narcotics and Narcotic Addiction*. Springfield, Illinois: Charles C Thomas, Publisher, 1962.

Moscow, Alvin, *Merchants of Heroin*. New York: Dial Press, 1968.

Index

FROM
HERN
BRARY